Once in Kazakhstan

Once in Kazakhstan

✦

The Snow Leopard Emerges

Keith Rosten

iUniverse, Inc.
New York Lincoln Shanghai

Once in Kazakhstan
The Snow Leopard Emerges

iUniverse books may be ordered through booksellers or by contacting:

iUniverse
2021 Pine Lake Road, Suite 100
Lincoln, NE 68512
www.iuniverse.com
1-800-Authors (1-800-288-4677)

ISBN: 0-595-32782-6

Printed in the United States of America

To Tania, whose love and support changed my life.

"Kazakhstan will become a Central Asian snow leopard...with its inherent elitism, independence, intellect, courage, nobility, bravery, cunning...persistent in conquering new heights...possessed of western elegance...and eastern wisdom."

—*Nursultan Nazarbayev*
President of the Republic of Kazakhstan, October 1997

Contents

Prologue: A Reluctant Nation Emerges

"Good morning, comrades! This is Moscow, the capital of the Union of Soviet Socialist Republics. The time is 5:00." The radio announcer punctuated *Soviet Socialist Republics* as if he were introducing the starting lineup at a basketball game. I looked out from my hotel window at the majestic Alatau range of the Tien Shan mountains. I was not in Moscow, and the time was not 5:00 AM. I was at the Kazakhstan Hotel in Alma-Ata, the capital of the Kazakh Soviet Socialist Republic, one of the fifteen constituent republics of the Soviet Union.

It was late 1991 when I made my first trip to Kazakhstan. I was listening to Radio Moscow broadcasting in Russian from the nerve center of the once-mighty Soviet empire that ruled over the almost 17 million people of Kazakhstan. But I was two thousand miles from Moscow, fewer than two hundred miles from the eastern border of China.

Kazakhstan is the size of all of the other former Soviet republics put together, excluding the Russian Federation. Many Kazakhstanis boast, "You can fit five Frances into it." But for those in the West, Kazakhstan fills up the vast empty space on the map between China and the Caspian Sea. Indeed, Kazakhstan is a huge territory, more than a million square miles, but mostly of unforgiving steppe. It is the largest landlocked country in the world, fostering a continental climate with extreme weather patterns.

Because Kazakhstan was remote and sparsely populated, it was an ideal destination for exiles and for party bureaucrats trying to make a name for themselves. You may not know Kazakhstan, but you know Dostoyevsky, Trotsky, and Brezhnev, all of whom spent a portion of their lives in Kazakhstan.

The failed putsch in Moscow in August 1991 prompted other republics to ready frantically for independence. But Kazakhstan acted as if it were still part of the Soviet Union to the last, seemingly oblivious to the whirlwind of change around it. With the backdrop of these events, I was invited to join two other lawyers on a United States Information Agency program to Kazakhstan. I had studied Russian as an undergraduate in California and Soviet law as a law student at the University of Illinois. I had practiced law several years and worked as a consultant on projects in the Soviet Union. But no one could have foretold that my background and education would lead me to the Central Asian steppe to witness the disintegration of the Soviet Union.

Our mission was to work with the Kazakhstan parliament, known as the Supreme Soviet, on reviewing new business legislation—the beginning of a monumental task of building the legal infrastructure of a new nation. The head of the parliamentary committee on legislation summarized the magnitude of the parliament's task: "We are starting from zero."

During the visit, Alma-Ata held the last celebration of the October Revolution. As in previous years, red banners decorated the streets. As a token gesture to old-line communists, a very brief goose-stepping guard appeared outside the parliament building. But the communist slogans had disappeared, and so had the grand parades with formidable displays of military prowess.

The city creatively transformed the day into a celebration for Tokhtar Aubakirov, the first Kazakh cosmonaut. A crowd of 15,000, small by comparison with the obligatory appearances of prior years, showed up to honor Aubakirov and to watch the dancers in exotic Kazakh dress. The adjoining street was once called Stalin Street, but with Stalin's disgrace, the name was changed to Communist Prospekt. "Now we'll have to change the name again," one parliament member observed.

The celebration of the October Bolshevik Revolution reflected the precarious balance Kazakhstan was trying to maintain between the conservative forces and the emerging new generation of leaders. Although the Communist Party was dissolved in Kazakhstan in the wake of the failed August coup, the *nomenklatura*, the privileged party elite, continued to hold the reins of power—under the banners of capitalism and democracy rather than communism. As one Kazakh lawyer commented, "The same communists are still in power. They just have different business cards." The presence of Lenin still loomed large over the capital. Portraits of Lenin still graced the offices of members of the Supreme Soviet. Even Kazakh State University still proudly carried the sign over its entrance: "Learn According to the Precepts of Lenin!"

After it became clear that the remnants of the Soviet empire would not reemerge as a new confederation, the Supreme Soviet of the Kazakh Republic was left with no choice other than to vote for independence. On December 16, 1991, two weeks before the country to which Kazakhstan had belonged for seventy years dissolved, the Supreme Soviet voted to declare a new country: the Republic of Kazakhstan. There was little fanfare.

The declaration of independence presented Kazakhstan with huge challenges. Kazakhstan needed to develop its own tools of governance for a country possessed of vast natural resources—and an arsenal of hundreds of nuclear warheads. Once a puppet of the Communist Party, the Kazakhstan parliament needed new legislative initiatives to stabilize the economy and attract foreign investment.

Kazakhstan was one of the few republics that did not act riotously to jettison the past. Rather, with the former head of the Kazakhstan Communist Party, Nursultan Nazarbayev, at the helm, Kazakhstan plotted a moderate path to democracy and a free market. Nazarbayev pledged that Kazakhstan would give up its nuclear weapons. Kazakhstan firmly allied itself with Russia, but it was a relationship in which Kazakhstan was the poor stepchild. The Russian Federation charged ahead with its reforms, with little consultation with other republics on the effects of the reforms outside the borders of the Russian Federation. Nazarbayev also actively sought Western assistance to fill the void left by the dissolution of the Soviet Union.

Nazarbayev became the Administration's "fair-haired boy," as described to me by a State Department official. Kazakhstan's allure to the West was Kazakhstan's ability to maintain the delicate political balance between the two major ethnic communities, the Russians and the Kazakhs. Kazakhstan avoided the ethnic strife plaguing the political and economic development of other republics. The republic found a fragile harmony between the Russians and the Kazakhs and exhibited tolerance to its other ethnic groups.

The emergence of Kazakhstan as an independent state captivated my interest and motivated me to plan a return to Kazakhstan. The Fulbright program, which supports U.S. scholars and professionals in various academic disciplines and professional fields to lecture abroad, became the vehicle for my return to Kazakhstan. Two years after Kazakhstan achieved independence, the U.S. government offered me as a present to Kazakhstan, as a Fulbright Lecturer in Law.

My return to Kazakhstan revealed a new Kazakhstan. People of all ethnic backgrounds were struggling with the past, trying to make sense out of the Soviet era, while searching for a new way for themselves and for the country. Both major ethnic groups in Kazakhstan, the Russians and Kazakhs, were wandering the new political and economic terrain of the country, virtually lost in the monumental changes that had enveloped Kazakhstan. I became a witness to their search.

During my stay in Kazakhstan, I kept a journal, which I called the Almaty Journal, attempting to capture the challenges of everyday life in a new country searching for its identity. The Almaty Journal endeavored to provide glimpses of the path that the people of Kazakhstan were taking to develop a new identity for their country. This book, an edited collection of the Almaty Journal, is for readers who want an intimate view of the struggles of one of the countries molded from the remnants of the Soviet Union.

1

Old Silk Road Returns to Glory

September 1993

Another Trip to the Hinterlands

Kazakhstan gives new meaning to the word hinterlands. On a flight from San Francisco, a stopover in Frankfurt, Germany, means travelers are only about halfway to Kazakhstan's capital, which has now been renamed Almaty. I arrived in Almaty on Lufthansa after a ten-hour flight from San Francisco to Frankfurt and then an eight-hour flight, including a short stopover in Uzbekistan, from Frankfurt to Almaty.

Landing in Tashkent, Uzbekistan, I saw the flickering lights of a major city stretching for miles and miles below. They did not even give a hint that I was in one of the historic cities of Central Asia. After landing on the bumpy runway, we pulled up next to a plane painted in blue and white, with lettering that read "UZBEKISTAN." It became clear that I was no longer in the comfortable confines of my native California. The plane next to us was a remnant of the old Aeroflot fleet.

The brief stopover was a vivid reminder of the fragile balance between various ethnic groups in virtually all of the former republics of the Soviet Union. Some of the passengers' final destination was Uzbekistan. An older Uzbek man slowly moved down the aisle towards the exit. A Russian woman and her young daughter were sitting behind me.

"How was your trip?" the Uzbek man asked the little girl, trying to be friendly.

The girl smiled bashfully, and her mother politely chimed in: "We're not home quite yet."

Trying to humor his captive audience, the Uzbek joked good naturedly, "So, why are you making me leave?" meaning that, if we were not home yet, why would he have to get off in Tashkent.

A rotund middle-aged Russian woman in a generic flowery Russian dress stood behind the Uzbek in the aisle. Without provocation, she joined the conversation. She had no humor in her voice when she sharply exclaimed: "No, it's you who are making the Russians leave." She was referring to the mass exodus of Russians from Uzbekistan.

The exchange underscored the ethnic tensions that have taken firm root in this part of the world. Gorbachev's policy of glasnost inadvertently unleashed pent-up ethnic acrimony that had been subdued for decades or even centuries. During my last visit to Kazakhstan in 1991, I had pressed young Russians to tell me whether they had been the targets of prejudice or discrimination because they were Russian and whether they were anxious about their future. They had responded uniformly that the "nationalities question" was not of great moment to them.

After almost two years of independence, Kazakhstan is testing the mood of its people to determine whether ethnic issues have overtaken the other great issues of the day. It is not a question from which one can easily hide. Even in the post-Soviet era, all citizens 16 and older must carry an internal passport identifying their "nationality." The passport is the primary means of identification, and line five of the internal passport removes the guesswork about the nationality of the passport holder. Ethnic groups, such as Russians, Ukrainians, Germans, Jews, and Koreans, are listed as "nationalities." Nationality plays a central role in admission to educational institutions, job possibilities, career advancement, and access to privileges.

Kazakhs Coming Home

The ethnic question pervades business and personal relations in this part of the world. In Russia, it may be hard to distinguish between a Russian and a Ukrainian. In Kazakhstan, there is no mistaking a Russian and a Kazakh. Russians are European in appearance, usually with light features. Kazakhs are Asian in appearance.

I went to a good dinner with some folks from the U.S. Embassy and two Kazakh sisters, a doctor and lawyer, who were born, raised, and educated in Russia. Their family lived in Russia for generations, but, a few years ago, they decided to "come home." They described their renewed appreciation for minor comforts, for living among their own people, and for people pronouncing their Kazakh names correctly. They doubted they would have been able to rise above low-level positions in their fields in Russia.

About 3.7 million Kazakhs, or about one-third of the entire world population of Kazakhs, live beyond the borders of Kazakhstan. As many as 750,000 live in the Russian Federation. As they "return" to the land of their ancestors, will they seek to create a "Kazakh" nation to the exclusion of other ethnic groups? Or will this country be a Kazakhstani nation, an inclusive home to many peoples? One of the sisters suggested that more Russians would leave Kazakhstan if they could find some place in Russia to go. She did not seem displeased by this prospect. But the official position of the Kazakhstan government is not to encourage the emigration of the Russian population.

Underlying Tension

There is a persistent undercurrent of tension between ethnic groups. In mixed groups, Kazakhs and Russians will boast of interethnic harmony. But when you get Russians alone, they often tell a different story.

In a taxicab one night, two Russians picked me up. We struck up a conversation. After feeling comfortable enough to share their thoughts with an American, they started railing on the Kazakh population. The driver sharply remarked that "all the factories are run by Russians." And he added, "they wanted sovereignty...let them live in yurts." (Yurts are circular, domed portable tents used by Kazakhs, similar in purpose to the teepees of the American Indians.) He said that all of his friends were leaving, and "I am leaving just as soon as I can."

The ethnic Russian population, however, has not left Kazakhstan in droves—in contrast to the large migration of the Russian population from other Central Asian republics. The government recognizes that a wholesale exodus of Russians could spell economic disaster because Russians are concentrated in industry. There are 2.3 times as many Russians as Kazakhs in industry. And conversely, there are three times as many Kazakhs as Russians in agriculture. There has been no effort to rid Kazakhstan of its non-Kazakh populations.

◆   ◆   ◆

Images around Town Show a Country of Contrasts

Almaty has evolved since I was last in this remote capital almost two years ago in 1991. There has been no major overhaul of the city. The tall statue of Lenin still dominates a park across from the parliament building. As a young Kazakh told me, "It's still too early to tear down the old monuments." Even though many signs are only in Kazakh, Russian is still the language of the capital, and even young Kazakhs speak Russian with one another. More and more people are learning Kazakh, except the Russians, who, like Americans, are not very good at learning the languages of others.

Crowd gathers on Old Square Across
from the Parliament Building.

Almaty is a city of contrasts. Elderly Russian and Kazakh men wear their World War II medals, earned fighting for a country that no longer exists. Kazakhstan sent 1.2 million men to the front during the War. The Soviet government evacuated 140 enterprises and one million citizens to Kazakhstan. The new Kazakhstani soldiers wear the old Soviet uniforms, hammer and sickle and all.

There is a huge monument for the soldiers who fell in the October Revolution and World War II. It is known as the Memorial of Glory and is located in the park named after 28 Guardsmen who served in the Panfilov Division during World War II. Panfilov Park has carried four names since it was originally named Pushkin Park in 1899 in honor of the 100th birthday of the Russian poet. Despite its newfound independence, Kazakhstan has left the Memorial of Glory intact. Before the dissolution of the Soviet Union, newlyweds came to this monument on their wedding day to pay their respects and place flowers at the monument. This tradition continues to thrive in the post-Soviet era. Russians and Kazakhs alike steadfastly observe this tradition.

Wedding party at the
Monument of Glory.

Panfilov Park is also home to
the Saint Voznesensky Cathedral,
built between 1904–1907.

Marching to the Beat of a Central Asian Drummer

Present-day Almaty is strikingly different than Moscow—but much the same. I can turn on Moscow radio, listen to Moscow television, and almost everyone in this capital speaks Russian. Almaty suffers from the same lack of public services as Moscow. The garbage trucks have not picked up the trash in more than a week. There was no gas for the trucks.

There are differences, not the least of which is the temperature. In Moscow, the temperature is already dropping into the forties; here it is still in the eighties during the day. In Moscow, there is a palpable resentment of those who are recently "moneyed," not only the mafia, but also those who earned their money through legal means. BMWs and Mercedes are abundant here in Almaty, but the owners are not subject to the same resentment as in Moscow.

Kazakhstan is actively exploring relations with other countries. Turkey is making a big play in Central Asia for influence, spending considerable money in the region. You can watch Turkish television here. But the government refused Turkey's suggestion to switch Kazakhstan to the Latin alphabet.

There is the Far Eastern influence, particularly the Chinese, the largest trading partner of Kazakhstan. But Kazakhstanis are wary of China. If China wanted to "borrow" some land, this country of not even 17 million could hardly deter China with its population of more than a billion. Strobe Talbott, U.S. Ambassador-at-Large, was recently here to discuss security issues. Take a look at the map. This landlocked country is virtually indefensible. China poses a threat to Kazakhstan, but it is not alone. Russia, or even Afghanistan or Iran (through Tajikistan), could present a threat to Kazakhstan.

The largest embassy in Almaty is that of Iran, which hungers for political and cultural influence in Central Asia. In Kazakhstan, the women do not wear the chador, the traditional Moslem veil. But the Kazakhs are nominal Moslems. They are proud of their religious heritage, although they drink hearty amounts of vodka and don't pray. For many of them, being Moslem is being a good person.

And of course, Western influence is omnipresent. The music, the soap operas (the U.S. soap, *Santa Barbara*, is especially popular), and the dress all point to a Western influence. Many people have asked me questions about life in the U.S. based on a rerun of *Santa Barbara*. I doubt that the producers of *Santa Barbara* know that people in Central Asia would view the American way of life through the prism of a soap.

◆   ◆   ◆

Even Stairs Are a Challenge

Upon my arrival to Kazakhstan, I moved into an old Soviet-style hotel, the Issik, clean but modest. The three stars emblazoned over the entrance belie the meager accommodations. I was certain that the Automobile Club was not responsible for the rating, especially as I looked for the phone jack (to connect my modem through electronic mail to the outside world). The jack had been removed, but I did find an unfolded condom—I guess they hadn't cleaned the corner in a while.

Outside the hotel, young men in their twenties and thirties park their fancy cars and chatter with one another for hours on end. Young boys equipped with buckets and rags offer car-washing services. Most of the hotels around town seem to have this same portrait of Almaty living: young boys contributing to the emerging market by washing cars.

On the inside of the Issik, a few slot machines have crept into the lobby, like most all of the other hotels in Almaty. The small "lobby" has a marble floor. The stairwell leading to the upper floors consists of five steps of varying shapes and unequal heights. The next to the last step from the top is of the oversized variety, whereas the last stair, as I quickly learned, is a miniature model, about half the size of the others. Out of habit, as I stepped on the last stair, I expected about six more inches of stair. The first couple of days of my stay, I stumbled every time. The workers must have built the stairs with uneven heights on purpose, to provide entertainment. I was not disappointed as I watched newcomers to the hotel attempt to master the stairwell…with about the same level of success as I experienced.

Cultural Particularities

There are still some cultural particularities that strike me as peculiar, probably revealing my Western slant on things. It puzzles me how the European (or is it Kazakh?) tradition of taking off one's shoes and putting on slippers survives in houses that are infested with cockroaches and a myriad of other bugs. And it constitutes a terrible faux pas to go into a cockroach-infested apartment with shoes on.

Kazakh men sit on the streets in what looks like a very uncomfortable position. They squat with their bottoms almost touching the ground, fully extending their backs, presumably for balance. They sit like that for long periods of time, as if they were sitting in a yurt.

My descriptions may give the false impression that this place is somewhat uncivilized. It is not. Buses run, people work, and there is plenty of food. The Central Market is not unclean, and it compares favorably with produce markets I have seen in parts of the U.S.

◆   ◆   ◆

Ambivalent Welcome

The institution of higher learning with which I am associated is the Kazakh State Academy of Management. The embassy found this host institution, which has experienced a huge turnover in faculty and staff. Like many institutions, it is also undergoing an identity crisis. The Academy was previously known as the Institute of the Economy, then the Kazakh State Economics University, before settling on its current name. The Academy is a "Kazakh" institution, which suggests that the Academy is only for Kazakhs, rather than a "Kazakhstani" institution, which would suggest that the Academy is for all ethnic groups living in Kazakhstan. Despite the name, the students are of both Russian and Kazakh ethnic backgrounds.

I have traveled extensively within the former Soviet Union. In my travels, I have been treated either like royalty or cast aside like an intruder. It is becoming increasingly clear that this trip falls into the latter category. Sharzada Akhmetova is the head of the international department, charged with the responsibility of looking after foreign visitors at the large Academy of Management. She started her job a few days before I arrived in the country and cannot tell me what course I am supposed to teach, or even when classes are set to begin.

Sharzada, like many working in the academic world in Kazakhstan, is underpaid and overworked. She calls me every few days to find out how I am doing. Although she offers a sympathetic ear, she has neither the authority nor the inclination to assist in resolving these problems.

Children Return to School—to Learn How to Add on Abacuses

I went into a store to see what supplies were available to the children returning to school. The major store, Children's World, sells not only notebooks, paper, and pencils, but also abacuses for math class. Schools must be preparing the children to work in government stores, which continue to use abacuses to add up the prices of products. Small, inexpensive calculators have appeared in Almaty, but the adding machine of choice is still the abacus.

Many Kazakh parents are in a dilemma. They want their children to learn Kazakh, but the best schools are still Russian-language public schools. Although Kazakh is written using a modified Cyrillic script, it is a Turkic language, not even a distant relative to Russian. Kazakh was written using an Arabic script until 1928, when it was replaced with a Latin script; then, in 1940, Stalin forcibly introduced the Cyrillic script. Turkey has encouraged Kazakhstan and other Central Asian republics (whose languages are also Turkic) to return to a Latin script. But Kazakhstan resists radical shifts and will not likely make any changes.

Housing Challenges

The Academy tried to convince me to take a place that was expensive and closer to the Chinese border than the center of town. I declined. Landlords have doubled prices around town and, in some cases, have demanded even higher rents. Those who were in Almaty just a few months ago related to me that I could "live like a king" for $100 per month. I have now learned that kings live in squalid conditions. For around $250 per month, it is possible to find an apartment…far out of town. Those who want to live near the center in a decent apartment must plan on spending $400 or more.

My problem is that most landlords want at least a one-year lease, and they all demand payment for the year in advance and in cash. In the U.S., I would feel ill at ease with more than $200 in my pocket. Under local custom in Almaty, I have to walk around with a couple thousand dollars in cash when I pay the rent for my apartment.

Looking for apartments has been an interesting process. I have enlisted the services of two brokers, Gulmira and Monas, who charge three percent of the rent for the entire term of the lease. They have escorted me to view more than ten apartments. Those showing us apartments have been more than hospitable. A few days ago, we went to see three apartments, none of which was adequate for my purposes. The people who showed us the last apartment were some young people in the throes of a small gathering with some friends. They had already started with some vodka and refused to let us leave until we joined in the festivities. So we stayed, and I drank more than my annual quota of vodka before we left.

In meeting the local crowd, I am left with the impression that the allure of foreigners has worn off since my last visit to Almaty in 1991. In my two-year absence, foreigners have become a common sight. Unlike a couple of years ago, when a flood of Westerners invaded Moscow and Leningrad, underlying resentment against Westerners is not apparent in Almaty. One potential landlady hoped to pocket ten times her paltry salary by leasing me her own apartment and living with her parents. She complained of low wages despite her PhD-level education, but even she did not blame foreigners for her woes.

Construction...Soviet Style

In Almaty, most people live in multistoried apartment complexes. Most of the apartment buildings do not exceed seven stories because of the earthquake danger and because an elevator is not required in buildings with fewer than eight stories. There are single-family dwellings in Almaty, but these generally are not desirable because they do not include some modern amenities, such as toilets, inside the house.

A local businessman has been building a house just outside the city. The house has been under construction for almost three years. He wanted to show me the house. We gathered in his BMW and took a ride to the house, located in the foothills on the way to the mountains.

Many of the houses in this development are in secured compounds, and all are very impressive. The work on my host's house was very solid, and the house itself was very impressive. But the stairs were uneven. Many were not the same size, and some stairwells were probably twice as steep as their American counterparts. I was never very good at architectural drawings, but, before I built a three-story house, I would want to check my calculations for the stairs.

Cholera Outbreak

Since Almaty is now a major trading center for East and West, merchants from China, Pakistan, and other areas bring their goods and produce to Almaty—and introduce various diseases into the population. The authorities closed the local produce market because of an outbreak of cholera, the one immunization I did not get before I left the U.S. In any event, immunization is only about 50 percent effective. With the outbreak of cholera, the authorities somehow found some gas for the garbage trucks to collect the refuse.

The cholera outbreak mobilized the local administration. Restaurants and cafes closed for a thorough cleaning. The airport was closed, ostensibly for "technical reasons." Rumor had it that the authorities acted to prevent people with cholera from leaving or from coming into the country with the disease. Rumor also had it that passengers needed to show a clean bill of health or other certificate to get on the plane. Another rumor blossomed: the water in the city was to be turned off to prevent further spread of the disease. Rumor is the staple of good conversation—even in the post-Soviet era, reliable information is hard to come by. Local custom requires those hearing a good rumor to embellish it and pass it on.

◆   ◆   ◆

The International Fair Comes to Almaty

The Karkara celebrated its centennial in Almaty. The Karkara is an international fair established by decree on January 29, 1893, in an area near Almaty. At the time of the Silk Road, an ancient trade route that linked China with the West, the Karkara provided a place to display and sell wares. The fair reopened in 1992 after a 62-year hiatus. This year, it attracted many U.S. companies, including Xerox and Lotus Development. The organizers set up some tent-like yurts to show off folk art. At the fair, the yurt with the most people was the one with Barbie dolls. Yes, yurts and Barbie dolls—this is quite a place.

Yurt in snow.

Billboards on the fairgrounds recount the rich history of Karkara. The "official" history is a good example of Soviet double talk. The billboards say that the fair was closed in 1930. Why? Because "with the strengthening and development of governmental and cooperative trade," the fair was no longer "advantageous" or "expedient." Who wrote this stuff? This is the 1990s, not the 1950s!

Entrance to the Karkara.

In 1930, Stalin enforced his policy of collectivization throughout the Soviet Union. Forced collectivization exacted an extraordinary toll from the Kazakh population, who were nomads dependent on their herds of sheep and goats for their livelihood. The party chief at the time, F.I. Goloshchekin, implemented harsh measures to transform the Kazakhs into collective farmers. The results were catastrophic. Within two years, the Kazakhs lost more than half of their population. As Kazakhs starved to death or died from diseases related to malnutrition, the population in two years shrank from more than 4 million to just 2 million. A Kazakh historian gives the following perspective on the events of 1931–1932:

"'Attack the nomads and annihilate them, like wolves.' Such was the adage of the Chinese in the middle-ages on how to deal with the ancestors of the Kazakhs. Military leaders of the Middle Empire did not succeed then in carrying this out. The party leader of Kazakhstan, Goloshchekin, turned out to be more successful in the 1930s. According to his convictions, the Kazakh nomadic environment was not compatible with socialist ideas. Socialism could prevail only with the transition of the Kazakhs to a sedentary way of life with subsequent collectivization. He succeeded in this. For these couple of years, 52 percent of the Kazakhs, that is, 2.2 million people perished from famine and epidemics, and 15 percent left the republic. This period went down in the history of Kazakhstan as the 'Goloshchekin Genocide.'"

One elderly man recently recounted to me this period when he was growing up in Alma-Ata. According to his description of this tragic time, there was utter social panic on the streets. Goloshchekin was as impulsive as Stalin, "but more primitive." Goloshchekin's approach to transforming the Kazakhs was, in effect, to issue a decree that "you are no longer nomads." The government removed any means for the Kazakhs to support themselves. The elderly man vividly recalled how every morning corpses were gathered onto carts and hauled away. It was a calamity of unparalleled proportion in the history of the Kazakh people.

Kazakhs rarely discuss the near genocide of their people. There is a monument of Lenin in every city in Kazakhstan. There are monuments to the war dead during the October Revolution and World War II (known as the Great Patriotic War). But there are no memorials to this great tragedy of the Kazakh people.

◆   ◆   ◆

The Currency Is Chaotic

The currency is a mess. The Soviet rubles in circulation in Kazakhstan are no longer legal tender in Russia. Russia has introduced its own currency, the Russian ruble. Thus, there are two exchange rates: one for "Soviet" rubles and one for "Russian" rubles.

Earlier this month, Islam Karimov, the president of neighboring Uzbekistan, had announced that, in a matter of weeks, there would be a new currency for both Uzbekistan and Kazakhstan. The policies of the central bank in Moscow have effectively forced the other countries from the ruble zone, and the hope of one currency for all of the republics of the former Soviet Union is a fleeting memory. The introduction of a new currency would mean more trade barriers and economic problems that these newly independent countries do not need, but mastery over the currency is one of the essential attributes of sovereignty. If Karimov's statement is correct, it is puzzling that Kazakhstan would tie itself to Uzbekistan, not one of the more progressive countries in the region.

After Karimov's posturing, the governments of Kazakhstan, Uzbekistan, Russia, Armenia, Belarus and even the politically unstable Tajikistan signed an agreement for a new ruble zone. None of the commentaries in the local press were very favorable or gave much possibility for the new zone to survive. Nevertheless, the meeting underscored the progress that the Commonwealth of Independent States, the CIS, had made since it was founded in 1991 as a loose confederation of some of the former Soviet republics.

The CIS was essentially a fiction used to put the final nail in the coffin of the Soviet Union. No one gave much chance for the CIS to survive even a year. Each of the newly independent countries has dealt with the political and economic fallout from the demise of the Soviet Union, and, to some small extent, these countries realize that they may need each other—at least for a while longer. Anyway, the leaders of the CIS are the "good old boys" who ran the Soviet Union. Who are Kravchuk, Yeltsin, Aliyev, Shevardnadze, Nazarbayev, and friends? They are the folks who ran the "evil empire."

Handling Currency Is for Those Deft at Counting Money

During the Soviet era, Kazakhstan was shamelessly exploited. There were almost 500 nuclear detonations on the territory of Kazakhstan. The Aral Sea is the site of one of the world's greatest ecological disasters. Kazakhstan is still a dumping ground for Moscow—for old Soviet rubles, rubles that are no longer legal tender in Russia. The Russian Federation ceased using Soviet rubles in July 1993; they only accept 1993 Russian rubles. In effect, Kazakhstan has its own currency: the old Soviet currency.

Handling money is an art. There are many denominations. The exchange rate is about 2,200 Soviet rubles to the dollar. They do not have coinage, so every denomination is a bill, from a one-ruble note on up, including 3-, 5-, 10-, 25-, 100-, 200-, 500-, 1,000-, and 5,000-ruble notes. In contrast, in the U.S., there are essentially four bills in wide circulation. In Kazakhstan, they have ten bills in wide circulation, and none of them is worth very much.

In any store, all of the slots in the cash register have long since been exhausted, so the women behind the counter simply line up the various denominations behind them. Like rotting fish on a pier, the old stale currency lies on the counter. And Soviet money can't be used anywhere else in the former Soviet Union, except in the south in Tajikistan, which is in the throes of military conflict.

The exchange rate is plummeting. Now in September, 1993, it is about 2,200 and more for Soviet rubles. By comparison, about 1,200 Russian rubles equal a dollar. Among several former Soviet republics, there is an "agreement" about a new ruble zone, which should cause the old Soviet rubles to plummet in value. (In the few weeks since I have been here, the value of the Soviet ruble has dropped precipitously from 1,400 to 2,200 per dollar.)

In 1992, Kazakhstan checked in with an inflation rate of 2,000 percent; in the first half of 1993, the inflation rate slowed to an annual rate of 600 percent. But, as my friends have told me, wages have not kept pace with inflation. The purchasing power of a ruble at today's wages is about half of what it was just a few months ago in the spring.

◆   ◆   ◆

How Businesspeople Are Coping…with Difficulty

In this chaotic economic atmosphere, new entrepreneurs are trying to cope. Mantai Tulegenov is the managing director of a large construction company in Almaty. Unlike most companies, Tulegenov's company is not involved solely in trading products. His company actually builds something. He readily recites the challenges associated with his construction business, not the least of which is obtaining materials from traditional supply sources in Russia.

Tulegenov recounts some of his latest challenges. "Maybe it is even funny for you, but it takes one and even two months to send money." And what about supplies? Tulegenov's company has worked with a metal factory in Russia. He recounts how his company paid for ten railway cars of metal in January, 1993. Although the company had a good relationship with the factory, the factory could not make the shipment for more than three and a half months because the Russian government imposed customs duties, prohibiting the factory from shipping the metal. The factory finally shipped the metal in April, but in the meantime the price of the metal had risen from 30,000 rubles to more than 100,000.

Tulegenov even imports nails from Russia because he cannot source them locally. The republics of the former Soviet Union were tightly integrated, and the dissolution of the Soviet Union could not wean Kazakhstan from its dependence on other republics. Like many Kazakhstanis, Tulegenov refers to Kazakhstan as a former colony of Russia.

"Because our republic was, to put it mildly, a colony of Russia—that is, Moscow, only the extraction and refining industry developed in the republic. We have virtually no machine-building. For us, all of the final manufacturing of products is done in Russia, and therefore the economy of Kazakhstan is closely connected with the Russian economy. At the present time we have become a politically free republic, but economically we cannot [say that], because our economy without the economy of Russia cannot move. Therefore, we are always looking at the political stability of Russia. If everything is fine in Russia, then our economy will develop normally."

Tulegenov believes that economic prosperity will diminish the importance of any festering ethnic problems. As he says, "We Kazakhstanis want to live in political stability irrespective of nationality. We need to live in peace and friendship—whether Kazakhs, Russians, or some other nationality. The important thing is that they are Kazakhstanis, so they believe in their republic—so we together improve our economy, so we emerge as a rich republic."

Russian Stability Is Not a Foregone Conclusion

The political stability of Russia is on everyone's mind here because events in Moscow have always affected the situation in Kazakhstan. Last week, I went to two conferences, one on the economy and one on the legal infrastructure in Kazakhstan. Events in Moscow preoccupied both conferences. The stalemate between President Yeltsin and the Russian parliament sent Kazakhstani government officials scurrying. It's hard getting accurate news because Yeltsin is firmly in charge of the press—and all of the reports on Moscow television and radio (which are the main sources of information) reflect a pro-Yeltsin view. I just learned that Yeltsin shut down Parliament's newspaper in an utterly undemocratic move.

Economics 101—Kazakhstani Style

Each of the conferences echoed some of the same views as Tulegenov's. One leading Kazakhstani economist, A.K. Koshanov, described one of the basic problems of the economy in Kazakhstan. The government wants to regulate the prices of monopolists, but, although there may be free prices, there is no real competition. In Koshanov's words, Kazakhstan is "technologically backwards and industrially underdeveloped." Last year, Kazakhstan suffered a $2 billion trade deficit, mostly because of trade with Russia. The major export is, not surprisingly, raw materials. Raw materials as a percentage of exports have even increased in the past few years, from 57.6 percent in 1990 to 78.5 percent in 1992.

The country is in the depths of an economic recession. Production has dropped to 1971 levels. About the possibility of a new currency, Koshanov maintained that "we are compelled to join the new ruble zone, because we are not prepared to issue our own currency." In any event, Kazakhstan cannot remain in this monetary limbo. Kazakhstan must either issue its own currency, the *tenge*, which has already been printed and is in warehouses, or cast its lot with the new ruble zone of the "new type."

University of Washington economist Judith Thornton summarized the findings of the conference: the economy of Kazakhstan is "held hostage to the economic collapse of the Soviet Union." The economies of the republics of the former Soviet Union are more tightly integrated than those of the separate states in the U.S. Kazakhstan has tried to jump over a chasm in two jumps. According to Thornton, Kazakhstan should decide which side of the chasm to climb up: either to rebuild artificial links to Moscow or to develop an independent economy, free of the constraints of dealing with Moscow.

What Law?

The international conference for lawyers held across the street at the Academy of Sciences was of a similar tenor. Speaker after speaker emphasized the necessity of creating a stable legal infrastructure to attract foreign investment. Some joked that, whatever new legislation was passed in Moscow, one could expect the same in Kazakhstan two months later. Some speakers were critical of the new decree on creating, or actually recreating, foreign trade organizations, with monopolies on trading in certain commodities. Some suggested that Kazakhstan was returning to rigid state regulation and were especially concerned that lawyers were not consulted in connection with the decree of July, 1993. Local lawyers and law professors argued about the image Kazakhstan was projecting to the outside world by repealing recent enactments on concessions and foreign economic activity—without enacting a replacement law.

One representative of Price Waterhouse, an international accounting firm, opined that what the Kazakhstani government needs is a law on contracts. He overlooked the Kazakhstan Civil Code from 1963, which continues to be in effect. Americans may want to resist the temptation to jump in like cowboys to right the wrongs of the world—at least before knowing something about the local cultural and political landscape.

Rush to Kazakhstan Continues

Nevertheless, the rush to Kazakhstan continues. Several law firms are considering establishing offices in Almaty. All the big five accounting firms have some presence in town. Kazakhstan's economic prospects are bright—if it can harness its enormous natural resources. Oil experts estimate that Kazakhstan has 25 billion barrels of recoverable oil reserves, rivaling those of Libya or even the U.S. Kazakhstan has 98 percent of the former Soviet Union's reserves in chromium and 82 percent of the phosphorous reserves.

Earlier this year, Chevron had signed a contract to explore and develop the Tenghiz fields, with 6–9 billion barrels of recoverable oil worth more than $114 billion dollars over the 40-year life of the field. Chevron's contract was the largest deal of its kind since Alaska's Prudhoe Bay was opened in the 1970s. A multinational consortium, including Mobil Oil and Shell, are negotiating an agreement to assess the Kazakhstan shelf of the Caspian Sea, the reserves of which may even surpass the Tenghiz fields. These deals would be an enormous catalyst to the Kazakhstani economy.

Foreign investment is in its nascent states, but the economy is already beginning to see the effects. Trade turnover is about $2 billion, with China representing almost 22 percent of trade. The U.S. represents a meager 5 percent of trade. More than 150 joint ventures are operating, contributing not only 1.1 percent to the national economy, but also valuable capital, technology, and know-how. Most economists would agree with the assessment of Tulegenov, the construction company president, who put it simply: "What we need is hard currency, hard currency, and once again hard currency."

The Pepsi Generation Grows Old and Gray

The rush to Kazakhstan has left at least one former major player behind. The president of Pepsi personally built the relationship with the former Soviet Union. The first agreement was signed in the early 1970s, and Pepsi became the drink of choice in the Soviet Union. Pepsi made the largest impact on the country, more than any other Western company. The relationship grew and prospered for almost twenty years, until something strange happened. The Soviet Union went out of business.

I saw an old weathered Pepsi sign on the side of a building on Toli Bi Street. The sign looked like many other old signs peeling off buildings that no one cares to repaint. I think Pepsi is still a favorite drink in Moscow, but Pepsi is virtually absent from the shelves in Almaty. All the years and effort Pepsi spent building the relationship appear to have been for naught. I don't have any data, but my personal observation is that, although I have seen and drunk many other varieties of colas, I have not seen, let alone drunk, a Pepsi since arriving.

Weathered Pepsi sign on Toli Bi Street.

◆   ◆   ◆

A Place to Live…Finally

I moved into my apartment last week…and am very pleased. The two-room apartment is not in the center of town, but relatively close to both the center of town and the Management Academy. It costs $400 a month, about $250 per month more than I expected to pay.

The area is quiet. It is not the most desirable part of town, but not the least desirable. Almaty's most desirable regions are further "up," in the southern reaches of the city. The city is upside down. The mountains are to the south. When one gives directions, to go up means going south, and to go down a street means going north.

The apartment has a bedroom, a living room, kitchen, toilet, and separate bathroom, which is more than adequate for one person, but not for the family of four who lived in the apartment before me. The bathtub doubles as a shower and actually has a shower curtain, an innovation in this part of the world. Most bathtubs in the former Soviet Union are sans shower curtains, allowing a good portion of the shower water to flood the bathroom.

The bathroom also has what is called a washing machine, a distant relative of its Western counterpart. I first soak my clothes for about an hour in the bathtub with laundry detergent, which I brought from home. Then I rinse the clothes. In the meantime, I hook up a rubber hose to the bathtub spigot with the other end in the washing machine. I turn on the water in the tub and water flows into the washing machine. I add the clothes and turn the machine on. The machine gyrates and shakes as it washes the clothes. I rinse the clothes again and place them back in the tub, this time with no detergent. I then rinse the clothes again and place them on the balcony, if it is warm, or on lines in the bathroom, if it is cold outside. I then drain the water from the washing machine. I let the clothes dry sometimes for as long as two or three days.

The capacity of the washing machine is about a third of Western models, so I have to repeat this process many times. And I have an advanced model of the washing machines made in this part of the world.

All of the closets are packed to the gills with jars of food, from preserves to pickles, just in case of an emergency. All homes have similar stashes. Kazakh and Russian homes look similar, except that Kazakhs have their rugs on the floors and the walls. Russians generally keep the rugs on the floor. My landlords are Russian.

The kitchen is small. I have to light the gas stove with matches. I actually have two refrigerators, one in the kitchen and one in the hall. Food is a major pastime in Kazakhstan, and many Kazakhstanis find it desirable to have an extra supply of food for guests who may drop by at any time.

Shopping is a daily activity, because nothing keeps. Preservatives have not hit the market. The bread is good on the first day, but you should not leave it for more than a couple of days unless you want to create a monster. I have learned not to leave bread in the bread bin for a couple of days. You haven't seen such grotesque forms of mold unless you have seen bread sitting for more than a couple of days in Almaty. My shopping burden may be eased soon, as rumor has it that a Western-style supermarket will open in town this week, which would fall on the heels of the gala opening of an Adidas store in the center of town.

I live on the third story, an important factor for safety. The first floor apartments around town all have bars on their windows, because petty crime is a way of life in Almaty. Like most apartment complexes, the common areas are dismal affairs, dirty and dark. But outside my door, there is one rarity, a working light bulb.

Even though it is very clean, the apartment has more than its share of bugs. I've never seen so many varieties of bugs. Almaty is not for those with a distaste for bugs (read cockroaches); lines (when I went shopping for the first time, I bought 6 eggs and 200 grams of cheese—it's a start, but I balk when the lines are more than ten people); or locks on doors (good doors have at least three locks—I have three locks on my outer door).

Attempted Seduction or Friendly Neighbor?

I heard a knock at my door this past week. I wasn't expecting any visitors. When I approached the door, I recalled a German businessman who was beaten severely when he answered a knock at his door not long ago. I opened the inner door (I have an inside door and an outside metal door) and looked through the peep hole. I saw a strange woman standing in the hall. I didn't know her and went back to preparing my meal without saying a word. A couple of minutes later, the bell rang. I looked through the peep hole again. I saw a woman struggling with her keys and a loaf of bread, which kept dropping out of her hands as she tried to put her key into my neighbor's door.

"How can I help you?" I said through the door.

"Open the door," the voice on the other side of the door demanded.

"I don't know you," I replied.

"I don't know you either," she said. I went back to cooking.

Then the telephone rang. The woman's voice came through the receiver without the usual static. She was the woman in the hall, my neighbor. "Why didn't you help me? You should have opened the door." I apologized, explaining that she did not tell me she was my neighbor. I told her I would come over in a little while and introduce myself. She had learned from my landlord that I had moved in.

A little while later, while dinner was cooking, I went over to introduce myself to Olga, my neighbor, who is in her thirties. She is a single mother with a young daughter. She may have been attractive when she was younger, but then again maybe not. She started to put some tea on. I told her I just came over to introduce myself. She sat on the cushioned bench next to me in the kitchen. Her eyes were completely dilated. She sat close, very close, and displayed a mouth that would be the delight of any gold miner, but the scourge of any good dentist. I had to get out of there. Forget being polite, I had to get out of there. I told her it was a pleasure, indeed a real pleasure, and left. She called later that evening, but I feigned an excuse. I have yet to get together with Olga. It can wait.

◆   ◆   ◆

American Influence

American influence pervades the country. Both the two Moscow channels and the local channels frequently show American films and serials. I turned on the tube recently and on three channels there were three American films. I watched the last part of a *Planet of the Apes* movie. In some countries, they use subtitles, which help the viewers learn English. Here, they dub over the English, and most times the same Russian-speaking interpreter speaks over all the voices, for all the men, women, and children. There may be six people speaking, and the male interpreter speaks all of their roles, in one monotonic voice.

Western goods are aplenty in Kazakhstan. Mars and Snickers bars are particularly popular in the kiosks. It is strange to have Smirnoff vodka in a country that used to occupy the quality position in the U.S. with the Stolichnaya brand. A bottle of vodka costs under $4, slightly more expensive than orange juice, but much more readily available. With the average monthly salary of about $50, these goods should be out of reach of many. With countless kiosks lining the streets, each selling 5–10 different kinds of vodka, the men of Kazakhstan have somehow found a way to afford these goods.

The kiosks display U.S. goods—alongside Israeli, German, and Turkish wares. (Chinese goods, especially clothing, have the reputation for being cheap and literally disintegrate on the way home from the store.) But America has the name, and U.S. companies have been eager to make inroads in this country, in which the economy will rapidly expand in the coming years.

The programming on television breaks for commercials almost at random. And for a country that did not have advertising during the

Soviet era, the plethora of advertising is not an entirely welcome change. American companies are dusting off their old commercials, some of which are prohibited in the U.S. Kent has a commercial showing young business execs jumping into a billboard advertising Kent cigarettes, transforming them into water skiers. Then there is a strong steady Russian voice—"Kent—pleasant…Kent—that is America." Lucky Strike's commercial is in a similar vein: "Lucky Strike—the real American in Kazakhstan—an American original."

Moscow used Kazakhstan as a dumping ground for nuclear testing; now some tobacco companies are using Kazakhstan as a dumping ground for their cash cows, which is alright if we're talking about old computers—but cigarettes? Phillip Morris recently purchased the Almaty Tobacco Factory in the first major privatization in the country. With shrinking markets in the U.S., Phillip Morris is attacking markets abroad, and Kazakhstan is an easy target.

Advertising for Goods and Mates

There is almost nonstop advertising on local television. The commercials consist of a pretty Russian or Kazakh woman seated behind a desk, reading advertisements for various products for half an hour at a time. Radio advertising is of a similar ilk.

Moscow television similarly has an avalanche of commercials. It is now advertising trips to Hawaii. There are some people making lots of money as the economies in this part of the world ready for prosperity.

The local Almaty newspapers also advertise everything imaginable. The ads promote various goods and services, including apartments, but they omit the price. The prospective purchaser needs to call to ask the price.

The newspapers even carry personals. Some identify their "nationality," their ethnic background; some don't. Here's a quick sampling:

- She: Mixed: father is a Tatar; mother is a Russian, 40 years old, 5'2", ordinary, grown daughter, has home, wants to meet a man, profession does not make any difference. Details at a meeting.

- She: Serious girl wants to meet businessman, well-to-do, young man, nationality does not make any difference. About myself: 18—5'5", wise, demanding, with a strong character and a realistic view of life. In a man, I value a mind, generosity, practical, the makings of a leader, but not a slave-driver. Your photo and telephone will speed up a meeting.

- He: Tall, reliable, attentive, hard-working, not devoid in attractiveness, non-smoker, young man, 21—6'2", European nationality, living with parents, but financially independent, wants to meet kind, tender girl 19–23 years old, without harmful habits. Marriage is possible after mutual understanding.

- He: Attractive man, Kazakh, from Almaty, 34—5'11", higher education, wants to meet Kazakh woman no older than 35, preferably with an apartment.

The personals give a snapshot of interethnic relations. There are probably not many Serbs who would accept a Croat mate or Azerbaijanis who would accept an Armenian. But here, even though the "nationality" question is an enduring issue, Kazakhs and Russians still maintain close friendships, and some even marry outside their ethnic group. The intermarriage rate is not high, but significant. About 8 percent of Kazakh men marry out of the fold, but only 3 percent of Kazakh women. As many as 20 percent of Russian men and 25 percent of Russian women marry a member of a different ethnic group, although not necessarily Kazakh.

◆   ◆   ◆

Killer Hospitality

I have received numerous invitations for outings to the country, reminding me of my first trip to the countryside outside of Almaty in 1991 in what became known as "Sam's Feast." It will soon become apparent why.

It was a crisp autumn day when we piled into the old Soviet model Lada and set out for the country. The three Americans sat in the backseat; our Kazakh hosts sat up front. Heading out of the city, we saw the small quaint houses with no plumbing—very Soviet, not abject poverty, but close to it. The houses finally gave way to beautiful countryside. We passed through Dzerzhinsky City and started an ascent up a steep mountain road.

It wasn't at all certain that the car was going to make it, and then there was this persistent noise from the trunk. It sounded like the whole back end was going to fall off. But the road was particularly bad, so we tried to put it out of our minds. Nevertheless, the driver, Murat, noticed our uneasiness and tried to allay our fears: "Don't worry about that. It's just a live lamb in the trunk." I looked at Peter Maggs, a fellow lawyer who speaks Russian. We both understood perfectly. But Phillip, the other American lawyer, not knowing Russian, was as much in the dark as the lamb in the trunk.

We arrived at this tiny village on the road to the pioneer camps; our hosts took our lunch from the trunk, and we named the lamb Sam. We tied him up while we took a walk through an "experimental farm," which uses all natural fertilizers. Our Russian host showed us around; he was a stocky man with worn skin showing his 52 years. He described the farm with pride running to his core. One of our other hosts was quick to ask our views on Marxism. Once convinced that he wouldn't offend us, he opined that Marxism was a good idea, and Lenin too was right, but only Stalin warped this idea. In fact, in a strange twist of logic, he urged the view that there were three stages to communism: socialism, capitalism, and fully developed capitalism.

We returned from our walk for the first of endless dishes of food. After a full meal, we were ready to prepare the next meal: Sam. Sam looked like he knew where we were going. We stepped just a few feet away from the door. Our hosts brought along a not altogether sharp knife to cut Sam's neck. They tied his legs together, and, as one held him down and the other held his head, they slit Sam's throat. It took much longer than I expected. I didn't watch that carefully and turned my eyes several times. The procedure was far from quick, as Sam kept on squirming; even when our hosts thought they were done, Sam's feet were still kicking. They went back and finally finished the job.

Our hosts boasted that they had seen many places in the world but no place was better than this village. We went for another hike, taking a chance to admire the high mountain peaks piercing the cloudless sky. We came back again to a huge meal. Sam looked different. Indeed, it was hard to connect what we had seen in the yard with what we were served.

Do You Believe in Snowmen?

I recently went hiking with a group of friends in the local mountains. We did not take lunch with us but decided that we would eat at a restaurant after our hike. We climbed to the top of a hill with a magnificent view of the mountains, on which there was fresh snow. I asked about whether there were any shelters on the trails and whether anyone lived in the mountains. One of the women said that there were no rangers, just "the snow people." I was intrigued. Who were these snow people? She told me that they were wild people. Well, I wanted to know what language they spoke. But I learned that they don't speak any language at all, as they are wild.

"What do they look like?" I inquired further.

"They are half man and half animal." She was matter-of-fact about her response, as if I were in the nineteenth century, asking someone about the automobile. Then I asked whether she has seen any of them. No. Were there any pictures? No. Any evidence? No.

"How do you know they exist?" I asked.

"Of course they exist, people have seen them," she looked at me with some exasperation.

It finally occurred to me that the Abominable Snowman lives here in Kazakhstan but under an assumed identity. Or possibly the Yeti of the Himalayas. Yeti are supposed to be apelike creatures that live at the edge of the snow line in high valleys of the Himalayas. They have been described as large creatures, covered in brown hair, which walk upright like humans. Footprints 6–12 inches long have been found. Various expeditions have failed to find Yeti. The Himalayas are less than a thousand miles away. Could Yeti have found their way to Kazakhstan? A great idea for tourist trips could be to invite Americans to go hiking in the local mountains in search of the snowmen of the Alatau Mountains.

A Trip to the Central Market and a Country Dacha

The family who rented me the apartment moved into another apartment in the center of town. The parents, Natasha and Sasha, are in their forties. They have two children, a son, Dima, and a daughter, Tania. Natasha, Sasha, Tania, and I went shopping. Because petty theft is widespread, Sasha parks his car in a "secured" parking lot several miles from where he lives. No one leaves a car overnight unless it is in a parking lot surrounded by a mesh fence. Most lots have 24-hour security guards or menacing looking dogs. Sasha uses the car only on the weekends, when he can get gas.

Our first leg of the trip was to the Central Market, which had opened up again after the cholera scare. The authorities had traced the source of the cholera to a planeload of Pakistanis. Apparently they quarantined the Pakistanis, but three escaped. They were caught again. The Market is relatively clean, as central markets go. There are no newly slaughtered camels like I have seen in Egypt. Prices are relatively reasonable, such as about 10 cents for a pear, except for some scarce products such as lemons, which cost about $2 each. I bought the pears, not the lemons.

After shopping, we drove to the country. I keenly listened for any strange sounds emanating from the trunk. Fortunately, there were none. The mountainous regions around Almaty are wild, magnificent, and unapproachable with their huge cliffs.

The rocky, mountainous terrain, as inhospitable as it is for humans, is perfect for brown bear, ibex, and the endangered snow leopard. The elusive snow leopard is particularly venerated in Kazakhstan, but it has been on the endangered species list of the World Conservation Union since 1972—there may be as few as 180 left in Kazakhstan of a world population of 4,500–7,500. The snow leopard is about 4–5 feet long with a tail almost three feet long. The long whitish-gray soft fur is perfectly suited for the bitter cold. The snow leopard has a majestic stride as it hunts for its prey as high as 19,000 feet above sea level in the summer and as low as 6,000 feet in the winter. Its prodigious leaping ability allows the snow leopard to pounce on its prey up to 15 yards away.

Because of the geology, the area around Almaty is seismically very active. It is one of the hottest spots in the world for earthquakes. Granite cliffs rise hundreds of feet from the valleys.

Panorma of Tien Shan Mountains with Almaty in foreground.

We went to the Almaarasan Gorge, southwest of Almaty on the Northern slopes of the Alatau Mountains. The terrain is rugged, so hiking is very difficult. Those who picnic in the area pull their cars off the one-lane highway and set up their picnic. We walked along the road, admiring the scenery, and then returned to the car to continue the outing at the Volkov's dacha, a summer home.

There appears to be a building boom of dachas outside of Almaty. A dacha is usually a modest affair, just a place to get away on summer weekends to relax and garden. Some residents, however, are building large dachas, two and three stories. The Volkov's dacha follows the modest model, the size of a walk-in closet. It has two very small rooms consisting of less than 250 square feet. The main attraction of any dacha is the garden. The Volkov's dacha has a garden for tomatoes, beans, various kinds of raspberries, strawberries, and other fruits and vegetables. Several pear trees and apple trees crown the garden. We picked some vegetables there and ate some of the fruit off the tree.

We went back to the Volkov's for dinner. Sasha had to return the car to the parking lot on the other side of the city and returned on public transportation…about an hour later.

Moving the Capital

The earthquake danger in Almaty caught the attention of the president. President Nazarbayev floated a trial balloon of moving the capital from Almaty to Akmola, formerly Tselinograd and the center of the Virgin Lands Campaign of the 1950s. I did not hear the official reason, but one reason (rumor) I heard on the street and reported in the paper is that there is a severe earthquake threat in Almaty. Indeed, earthquakes have destroyed the city twice, in 1887 and 1910. Nevertheless, if the seismic danger is the genuine reason, one has to wonder why Nazarbayev gets to move to Akmola, and the rest of us in Almaty, more than 1.3 million strong, have to stay in the earthquake zone.

A poll published in the paper reported that, not surprisingly, 71 percent of the people in Almaty do not approve of the move. (Strangely,

20 percent approve of the move!). Roughly 56 percent of the people surveyed in Akmola approve of the move.

These pronouncements make life interesting because the tradition of Soviet-speak continues. Everyone knows that the "earthquake hazard" is not the real reason for the possible move, but speculation runs rampant about the true reasons for Nazarbayev to consider the move. Some of the speculation is that Almaty is too close to China, less than 200 miles away. In the event of a war with China, Almaty, the center of government operations, would be overrun within hours. Kazakhstan is keenly aware of the threat posed by 1.2 billion Chinese at its doorstep.

Another factor may be to secure the capital in the north, where the ethnic Russian population constitutes a majority of the population. Some Russians have openly talked about secession from Kazakhstan. If Akmola were the capital, it would be very difficult for Russian separatists to demand secession of a part of the country in which the capital is located.

Whatever the true reason for the proposed move, the mere prospect of it generates enough press and attention for weeks of conjecture around the table.

2

The Battle for Kazakhstan's Soul

October 1993

Russia: A Democracy under Siege

"The White House is burning, the White House is burning," announced the television commentator on Russian television, referring to the Russian parliament building. Using footage supplied by CNN, he despondently told his viewers: "the whole world is watching these pictures on CNN."

Those were the images I viewed on television on the latest crisis in Russia. Even though we are close to Moscow, the information available in the U.S. about events in Moscow is as good as what Kazakhstan receives. During my stay here, I have received Russian television and radio as if I were in Moscow. I can also receive CNN. As the crisis unfolded, I desperately turned the television channels, trying to obtain current information. I talked to embassy personnel and government officials: all of their information was from CNN.

As the pace of new developments began to quicken, I even turned to my driver to learn whether he had heard anything. He heard about some of the events over MTV, the Asian version of which is broadcast here. The Moscow channels had precious little information, and, of course, with the attack on Ostankino—one of the Moscow stations—that source of information was curtailed.

On Monday, when Ostankino came back on the air, the pictures of the assault on the television station were vivid reminders of how tenuous the hold of democracy is in this part of the world. The television announcer told Yeltsin supporters that, if they wanted to go to the Mayor's office in a show of support for Yeltsin, they should dress warmly and bring tea.

As events unfolded, the various Moscow stations cut into CNN coverage. Even when the live CNN coverage from Moscow ended, CNN kept its cameras running and microphones on, allowing the Russians to use the transmission for Russian television. I probably watched the CNN transmission along with 150 million people in the republics of the former Soviet Union. The Russian announcer not only used the CNN pictures, but also commented on what the CNN reporter, Claire Shipman, was saying off camera as she was preparing for the next live segment. For example, when Shipman received the Reuter's report that 500 had been killed inside the "White House," she exclaimed (off of CNN live coverage, but broadcast live on Russian TV): "Jesus Christ, Jesus Christ." The Russian announcer then translated her exclamation over Russian television.

A Battle between the Past and the Future

The events in Moscow exposed just how shallow the roots of democracy are in the Russian Federation. The Russians are new to the ideals of democracy. Politicians unable to achieve their goals through political means eagerly picked up their guns in full view of the world.

This parliament originally elected Yeltsin, and Yeltsin chose Aleksandr Rutskoi, a war hero, as his vice president. As Rutskoi and speaker of parliament, Ruslan Khasbulatov, developed their own bases for support, especially with regional governments, they split with Yeltsin. Although Yeltsin may be the "most popular" politician in the country, he commands a confidence rating of less than 40 percent, according to the Institute of Sociology of the Russian Academy of Sciences.

Dissatisfaction with Yeltsin did not translate into popular support for Rutskoi or Khasbulatov. Nevertheless, they remained intransigent in their negotiations with Yeltsin. They expected to garner support for their bold "defense" of the Russian parliament building. Their initial success on Sunday, October 3, 1993, when their supporters overwhelmed government troops, emboldened Rutskoi and Khasbulatov. No significant additional support materialized for Rutskoi and Khasbulatov.

Kazakhstan quickly joined with Azerbaijan, Uzbekistan, Kyrgyzstan, Armenia, and Ukraine to declare their support for Yeltsin as a hopeful sign that some measure of stability might be restored. This declaration may be the first significant document that Armenia and Azerbaijan jointly signed since they became embattled in war in 1989. The support for Yeltsin from these republics is not surprising. Rutskoi has not endeared himself to these new countries. Rutskoi asserted Russia's interest in protecting Russians, wherever they are. For a new country such as Kazakhstan, in which almost 35 percent of the population is Russian, this extraterritorial claim causes great concern. But calm prevails in Kazakhstan today. There are no signs of any disturbances or demonstrations anywhere in Kazakhstan or the other former republics. The only sign in Almaty of the disturbances in Russia is that, in some quarters, people are riveted to their televisions.

The turmoil in Russia may derail some economic reforms. Several of the members of the Commonwealth of Independent States have been in serious discussions on a new ruble zone. The agreement on the new ruble signed last month is at risk. The parliament building of the lead country of the new ruble zone is ablaze.

I was in Moscow a couple of days after the defeat of the putsch of 1991 and visited the front of the White House, still adorned with barricades from those who defended democracy. Outside the White House, a man with a mustache was on the steps at the front of the White House, showing his guests how they had just beat back the reactionary forces. That man was Alexander Rutskoi. The Russian Federation now stands at the crossroads, and the man who defended the democratic ideal just two years ago in 1991 is holed up inside the White House, but now as a chief opponent of democracy.

There are other strange parallels between this putsch and that of October 1991. Rutskoi, a war hero of Afghanistan, was selected by Yeltsin as vice president. Pavlov, one of the chief architects of the 1991 putsch, was selected by Gorbachev as his prime minister only months before the coup.

The events in Moscow are not only a test for Russia, but for all of the republics of the former Soviet Union. As the president of Kyrgyzstan said, "this is a battle between the past and the future."

◆   ◆   ◆

The Kazakhs as Nomads

It is not easy to appreciate current events in Kazakhstan without a strong sense of history. Allow me to indulge in a short history lesson for those unfamiliar with the significant events and figures of Kazakhstan. Before the Soviet era, the Kazakhs were a nomadic people, assimilating into their own culture the influences of those peoples that happened through this part of the world. They trace their roots to Turkish tribes, who lived in the territory in the eighth century. Kazakh is a Turkic language, similar to modern Turkish, Azeri, and Uzbek. The history of Kazakhs as nomads even today plays a central role in Kazakh consciousness and identity.

Singer with a dombra, a Kazakh folk instrument.

On holidays, Kazakhs recall their past by setting up yurts, similar to those in which their ancestors lived on the steppe of Central Asia. Politicians argue against private ownership of land, based on their nomadic roots when their ancestors did not own land. The land was for everyone to graze sheep and goats.

A leading American scholar, Martha Olcott, suggests in her book *The Kazakhs*, "To be a Kazakh was to be a nomad." The nomadic life, however, was not one without toil and hardship. As one contemporary writer, Yuri Novikov, suggests in his article "The End of the 'Absolute Pasture'": "The life of a nomad is not so pleasant, so as not to try to leave it on the first opportunity." He quotes an Abkhazian saying with vivid imagery: "In the summer, animals provide us with fat, and in the winter drink our blood." The writer contends that the nomads created the steppe, and the steppe created the nomads, the ancestors of the Kazakhs.

Kazakhs look Mongolian. Some Kazakhs suggest that their people had a fair complexion and light hair before Genghis Khan conquered the area in 1219–1221. There has even been some archaeological support for this contention. Mongol domination of Central Asia endured until 1395. At the end of the fifteenth century and the beginning of the sixteenth century, the Kazakhs began to emerge as a separate people with a common language, culture, and economy. In the Semireche region of Kazakhstan, which extended from present day Almaty north to Lake Balkhash, the Kazakhs formed a political union, the Kazakh khanate. The Kazakh khanate was divided among three federations of tribes: the Great Horde in the Semireche region, the Middle Horde in central Kazakhstan, and the Small Horde in western Kazakhstan.

The Kazakh khanate reached its zenith at the end of the sixteenth century. The Kazakhs had gained control over the entire Syr Darya River basin, including the great cities of Turkestan, Tashkent, and Sarmarkand. But Kazakh domination was threatened from both Bukhara to the west and the Kalmyk state to the east. The Kalmyks posed the greater threat, systematically encroaching on Kazakh lands. By the end of the seventeenth century, the Kalmyks had taken almost all of southern Kazakhstan. By 1725, the Kalmyks captured the Syr Darya River basin in Southern Kazakhstan, forcing the Kazakhs to flee their ancestral pasturelands.

Genesis of the Relationship with Russia...a Lesson in Ambiguity

Kazakhs have had an ambiguous relationship with Russia for generations. The Kalmyk threat left the Kazakhs with little choice but to seek Russian protection. In 1728, the Small Horde in western Kazakhstan petitioned Russia for the Small Horde to come within Russia's protection. Russia approved the Small Horde's request in 1731, marking the end of an independent Kazakh state. In the next decade, members of various khanates of the Middle Horde also received Russian citizenship. The process of union with Russia both freely and by compulsion continued for another hundred years, until virtually all Kazakh lands joined with the Russian empire.

The voluntary union between the Small Horde and Russia continues to be a major point of departure in the relationship between Kazakhstan and Russia. For example, as the head of the Communist Party wrote in 1982 about this union, "It is impossible simply to interpret the motives and the entire complex process of the voluntary union of Kazakhstan with Russia, the beginning of which was 250 years ago—in October 1731. Notwithstanding the mercenary goals of tsarism, the opposition of reactionary feudal aristocracy and the Moslem clergy, the course of the indissoluble friendship with Russia, strongly supported by the working masses of the Kazakh and Russian peoples, prevailed."

When discussions turn to the current relationship between the Russian Federation and Kazakhstan, someone will invariably refer to the Kazakh entreaty to Russia in 1731 as the act that, for better or worse, joined Kazakhstan's fate with that of Russia. This historical orientation pervades the debate of current events.

Kunaev's Imprint

The single most important figure in modern Kazakh history is Dinmukhamed Kunaev. Kunaev died on August 22, 1993, and Nazarbayev, the current president, cut short a state visit abroad to attend the funeral.

Kunaev embodied the contradiction of serving Moscow while promoting the interests of a minor ethnic group in the Russian-dominated Soviet Union. He was a complex man, a staunch promoter of Kazakh interests, but a committed communist. He rose quickly in the Communist Party of Kazakhstan, primarily due to the failure of the Virgin Lands Policy. The Virgin Lands policy was inaugurated in 1954 to open up vast territories of land to cultivation. With slow implementation of the program, Khrushchev appointed his protégé, Leonid Brezhnev, as the First Secretary of the Communist Party of Kazakhstan in July 1955. But Khrushchev needed Brezhnev in Moscow, and Brezhnev packed his bags. As the Virgin Lands policy foundered, a series of first secretaries were appointed and dismissed. Kunaev was initially appointed at the end of 1959, but he could do no better than his predecessors to implement a failed policy. Kunaev lasted three years, before he too was removed on December 26, 1962.

Kunaev was, however, a resilient politician. After Khrushchev was ousted from the Party leadership for his failed economic experiments, Brezhnev emerged as the new Party leader in Moscow. In December 1964, the Moscow leadership turned to a Brezhnev protégé, none other than Dinmukhamed Kunaev, again to lead the Communist Party of Kazakhstan.

Kunaev reigned as Party chief in Kazakhstan for 25 years. He never forgot that he was an engineer, and, as many locals have told me, "He loved to build." He was devoted to the Soviet nation and eventually became the first non-Russian to serve on the Politburo for the entire Soviet Union. He was deeply proud of the Soviet influence in transforming the Kazakh people. In his autobiography entitled *About My Time*, Kunaev described Kazakhstan's place in the Soviet Union. Kunaev's own words best reflect his views of how Socialism was a "good thing" for the Kazakhs:

"What did the Kazakh people have before? They had a festive spirit, committing to memory thousands of lines of poems, and a gentle dombra [Kazakh folk instrument] in every yurt. But much more space should be devoted to what it did not have. There were no symphony orchestras, operas or ballets, or even elementary music books. There was no national art gallery, or even drawings other than ornaments. According to the tenets of Islam, any representation of the human form is a sin. The first professional Kazakh artists appeared in the Soviet time....And this long list of 'there weren'ts' was in a time when people had already been using locomotives, cars, airplanes for a long time, and radio and film had appeared!"

In his autobiography, Kunaev exudes pride over his Soviet-style accomplishments. He succeeded in developing the industries that the central planners in Moscow designed for Kazakhstan. Kunaev loved to build, and his list of accomplishments reads like a ticker tape of grandiose Soviet projects. His hand is evident throughout Almaty: the Parliament Building; the House of Pioneers and Students; Medeo, the winter sports stadium; Arasan, the baths; and, in honor of his mentor, Brezhnev Square, since renamed to New Square.

In Need of Heroes and Martyrs...and the Meaning of December

Most of the main streets in Almaty have been renamed to honor leading figures and events in the history of the Kazakh people, although virtually everyone refers to the old Soviet names. If I want to go to my apartment and I tell the cabby that I want to go to Toli Bi Street, he would look at me without comprehension. Even though it is not written anywhere on the road anymore, I need to say Komsomolskaya, the old name of the street.

Soviet era slogan on side of building:
"Peace, Work, Friendship, Freedom, Equality,
Brotherhood, Happiness"

The names of the other major boulevards have also been changed. Communist Prospekt is now Abylai Khan Prospekt. Soviet Street is Kazybek Bi Street. Most significant of all is the renaming of Mir Street, which in Russian means "peace," to Zheltoksan Street, which in Kazakh means "December."

The new government has a fascination with December, not because of the events leading to the declaration of independence in December 1991, but because of the events of December 1986, following the removal of Kunaev from office. After Gorbachev became General Secretary of the Communist Party of the Soviet Union in 1985, the official press launched a frontal attack on Kunaev. The attacks grew increasingly strident. On December 16, 1986, the plenum of the Central Committee of the Party in Kazakhstan sacked Kunaev.

The session of the plenum required only 18 minutes to remove Kunaev and replace him with an ethnic Russian, Gennady Kolbin, the leader of the Ulyanovsk Party organization. The events of the following two December days became a watershed for Kazakhstan. Even today, however, there are varying interpretations of the protests that ensued in the wake of Kunaev's removal from office.

The December Events

Winter came early in 1986, and there was already snow on the ground on Tuesday morning, December 16, when the plenum voted to place Kunaev on a pension. The news of Kunaev's removal prompted several hundred Kazakh youths to gather on Brezhnev Square across from Party headquarters the following morning.

The Square is now known as New Square and looks much as it did in 1986. It is a huge open area modeled after Red Square—but with all the subtlety of a ten-lane freeway. The Square even has a grandstand, made to look like a mock Lenin's Mausoleum (but without Lenin or his likeness). And the Presidential Palace, which was then the Party Headquarters, still stands ominously in the background. The protests on Brezhnev Square were utterly alien to the Soviet Union, and they caught the authorities by surprise.

By the early afternoon, the crowd had swelled to the thousands, possibly even the tens of thousands, according to some eyewitness reports. Estimates vary depending on who tells the story. Many of the people on the Square were simply curious about the "happening." When the president and even Nursultan Nazarbayev, who was then the premier of Kazakhstan, tried to address the crowd, they were drowned out with cat calls, whistles, and singing. Some in the crowd threw snowballs, while others taunted the soldiers guarding the podium. Young cadets from the police academy reinforced a cordon around the Square.

In the early evening, the Deputy Minister of Internal Affairs warned the crowd to disperse. The demonstrators refused. Darkness was falling when two columns of armored personnel carriers labored up Furmanov

Street towards the Square. Then the order was given…the soldiers set on the demonstrators with batons, provoking a violent response. Some of the demonstrators fled the Square, overturning cars and setting them ablaze on the streets of Alma-Ata. Others threw rocks, sticks, or anything else they could find at the soldiers. The disturbances had only just begun.

The demonstrations already had attracted the attention of Moscow. Representatives from various security forces from Moscow arrived in Alma-Ata and quickly determined to retake the square by force and remove the crowd in what they called "Operation Blizzard." Late at night, militia with dogs, billy clubs, and truncheons attacked the crowd, beating the demonstrators, even those already detained. Fire trucks were used to spray water on the demonstrators.

The next day, Thursday, December 18, there were further violent confrontations on the Square as the authorities determined to impose order. One demonstrator and one soldier were killed. There are some estimates that as many as 20,000 police and 50,000 soldiers and internal forces worked in Operation Blizzard.

It was evening when the final assault on the demonstrators began. The militia and special forces launched the attack. The crowd ran in all directions to escape the beatings. Those who fell were dragged away in military vehicles. Blood stained the snow on the Square. By 9:30 PM, after two full days, Operation Blizzard was complete.

The "December Events" claimed at least two lives on the Square, but even today the exact number of deaths is unknown. The head of a government commission looking into the December Events almost four years later has suggested that as many as 58 people were killed, but there is no hard evidence supporting this claim. Hundreds were injured, and more than 200 were hospitalized. Almost 100 protestors were sentenced to prison, and one demonstrator was sentenced to death.

The Need to Assess Blame for the December Events

The official press immediately blamed the mafia and underground nationalist organizations for the disturbances. More than 1,500 members of the internal police received commendations for "excellent service," and about 250 earned medals for Operation Blizzard.

Gennady Kolbin stayed in office as first secretary of the Party until 1989. When he left, there were calls to reexamine the December Events. A government commission was convened in 1990. Not surprisingly, the Shakhanov-Murzaliev Commission had a different take on the December Events. They concluded that "The actions of Kazakh youth in December 1986 in Alma-Ata and a series of regions were not of a nationalistic nature—it was the first attempt to exercise the rights guaranteed by the Constitution and declared by perestroika for free expression of a civic or political position. The deep reasons for the discontent of the youth came at its core from the low standard of living, social injustice and the cost of the command-administrative system....

"The immediate impetus for the action of the youth was the secret and insulting appointment of G. Kolbin as first secretary of the Central Committee of the Communist Party of Kazakhstan, which was taken as a crude dictate of the center for resolving issues affecting the vital interest of the population of the republic. There was particular outrage because of the obvious contradiction between the traditional command activities of the center and the proclaimed democratic principles of perestroika."

The Supreme Soviet endorsed the findings of the Shakhanov-Murzaliev Commission, passing a resolution on September 24, 1990. The Supreme Soviet virtually exonerated itself and all of the leaders of Kazakhstan, squarely placing the sole blame on Moscow. It faulted "a narrow group of people from the center" with the "inept decisions" associated with the December Events.

There continues to be considerable controversy over the Events, and the interpretations change with the shifts of the political environment. I think one journalist gives the most plausible interpretation of the

Events of December 1986: "The youth went out in December not 'for Kunaev,' or even 'against Kolbin,' but against the Goloshchekin genocide, the Brezhnev lies, against the very system...."

Nazarbayev Maneuvers through a Mine Field

This place appears to have all the ingredients for chaos, but President Nazarbayev has been able to maneuver through a mine field of ethnic tensions, economic travails, and political discord. Many openly wonder whether the harmony would remain if he were to leave.

Nursultan Abishevich Nazarbayev was born in 1940 in the village of Chemolgan, not far from Almaty. He is a Kazakh, but he speaks better Russian than Kazakh. After completing a technical school and completing his Party education, he worked in the city of Temirtau in the Karaganda Region, a northern region of Kazakhstan bordering Siberia. He worked for nine years as an iron worker at the Karaganda Metallurgical Combine.

But Nazarbayev did not become president like Lech Walesa of Poland. Like many leaders in the post-Soviet era, Nazarbayev rose to the presidency through Party ranks. In 1969, Nazarbayev got his start in Party work in Temirtau. He eventually returned to the Karaganda Metallurgical Combine as the secretary of the Party committee. By 1977, he was already second secretary of the Karaganda regional committee of the Party, and, in 1979, he landed a spot on the Central Committee of the Communist Party of Kazakhstan.

In 1984, Nazarbayev's stock began to rise rapidly as he became the Chairman of the Supreme Soviet of the republic. In June 1989, after Kolbin left the scene, Nazarbayev succeeded him as first secretary of the Central Committee. Then, the Supreme Soviet elected Nazarbayev as the first president in the history of the republic on April 24, 1990. Presidential elections were called on short notice in late 1991. No other candidate was able to obtain the requisite 100,000 signatures to earn a place on the ballot. Nazarbayev had virtually no opposition, and he received 98.8 percent of the 8.8 million votes cast on December 1, 1991, to become the first elected president of the republic.

◆   ◆   ◆

What If the Tables Were Turned?

I was walking with some friends on Lenin Prospekt. As we passed the slew of kiosks and street vendors, one of the young women in our group remarked how strange it was for her to walk with a foreigner. She recalled that, just a few years ago when she was in high school, she learned not to have any contact with foreigners. She, like many others in this part of the world, was utterly convinced that the path of socialism was the right path and that any visitors posed a threat to their way of life. I may not be the first to muse about what would have happened if we were the ones who turned out to be wrong, rather than the other way around. The people in the Soviet Union learned from childhood that we were the enemies, that any foreigners who visited the Soviet Union were subversives bent on the destruction of the Soviet Union.

But what if the tables were turned? What if it turned out that capitalism was only an instrument of the elite to suppress the masses? If there had been a war of the masses against the elite and socialism prevailed, how would we adjust to a new social, economic, and political system? If we close our eyes and try to imagine that everything that we embrace in our democracy were wiped away: the rule of law, the U.S. Constitution, our way of life, our culture, our standard of living, what images would arise? Then we would have a small notion of what the 285 million people of the former Soviet Union have had to do to adjust to their new reality as it evolved from glasnost and perestroika to independence for the former republics of the Soviet Union. The magnitude of the shift from political ideology in this part of the world is no less monumental.

◆　　　◆　　　◆

A Reception for an Academic

I went to the Institute of State and Law and met with the director, Erkesh Nerpesov, with whom I had spoken at a reception at the Embassy earlier in my stay. He has an enormous office befitting a director. I expected to stay for half an hour on a get-acquainted visit. The meeting was what I expected; what followed the meeting was not.

It was the seventieth birthday of one of the luminaries of Kazakhstan law, Professor Abdu-Ali Erenov. We had a small meal before the celebration, and I thought that I would leave. The vice director, in words that I think he sincerely meant, told me that, if I left before the celebration, I would not be welcome back. I took him at his word and stayed, and I was glad I did.

Almost everyone at the birthday celebration was Kazakh, and most of the speeches were in Kazakh. It was the first time since I arrived that I felt I lacked the language of power. Erenov is a gregarious man and taught me how to toast in Kazakh. He fought and was wounded at Stalingrad, losing his right arm. Nerpesov acted as the master of ceremonies. He followed a rigid order for those to give speeches in honor of the guest of honor.

The Academicians were of the first order. This title is reserved to those elected by the Academy of Sciences after a distinguished career. Ministers and deputy ministers in the government next lauded praise on Erenov. Professors were next in line and then foreign guests. I looked around. I was the only foreigner present. I was not prepared, but I think I lauded sufficient praise on the honoree, seeing as I had not met or heard of this man even an hour earlier. I got some laughs when I recounted how Erenov had taught me to toast in Kazakh, and then Erenov planted a big kiss on my lips (yes, that's what they do here).

After the official celebration, we retired for a meal in another room. The tables were set in a U-shape. There was another table at the top of the U, and people sat on both sides of the tables. There were probably 40 people sitting around the U—all of whom were men, with the exception of one woman. Even though there are a few women in government, the vast majority of the people in power in both business and government are men.

I sat next to the new Minister of Justice, Nagashibai Shaikenov. Shaikenov is youthful looking and is probably in his forties. I kept wondering whether he was indeed the minister. We had a brief but interesting discussion. He was recruited from Sverdlovsk (now Yekaterinburg), and he boasted that he planned to increase the ministry from 130 to 200 attorneys. Shaikenov will need as much assistance as he can get to build the legal infrastructure of this emerging country, and the people gathered around the table will likely be his most powerful allies.

Classes Begin

I gave my first lecture at the Management Academy yesterday. I have about sixty students, who are in their last year of their university training. Although they paid close attention to the lecture, I should not rest on my laurels. The novelty of an American professor teaching business in Russian may wear off. I have been told that attendance may drop off substantially. I asked the class how many of them had a working knowledge of English. Not even one student raised his hand.

The Management Academy is disorganized. I learned about my course from a secretary who could not give me even the most basic information about what I would teach, how many students I could expect in class, or even the title of the course. But she did give me the time and room number, information that proved useful. Fortunately, my students were better informed than I was. They told me the name of the course and when we were scheduled to meet again.

There has been a huge turnover in faculty. Teachers simply cannot survive on the salary that the school pays them. The average salary for an associate professor is less than the equivalent of $50 per month. If teachers have any practical skills, they leave academia for the private sector.

When I picked up a key from an old woman who gives out keys for classrooms and offices, she looked at me and exclaimed, "Oh, you must be one of the new ones."

"Are there many new teachers?" I asked.

"More than half of the teachers who sign for keys are newcomers," the woman replied.

In the meantime, I have agreed to teach another course at the Private Law College. The course will be an introduction to U.S. law for 110 students in the first-year program. The course is particularly relevant because Kazakhstan is now struggling with the very same issues with which America's founding fathers grappled more than 200 years ago in developing the legal institutions in the U.S. The students need not accept the U.S. approach, but the purpose of the course is to provide them with an understanding of the issues.

Knock, Knock... Who's There?

The students are not the obedient souls that one might expect, although the first impression is deceiving. As the teacher enters the lecture hall, all students rise and wait for the teacher to instruct them to be seated. But there the facade ends. Many students come to class late because of—as one student remarked—"problems with transportation." When students arrive late, they invariably knock on the door. There may be 60 or even 100 students in class, but students coming late knock on the door, as if they were entering a private apartment. There is a brief pause, and then they pop their heads in and say "May I?" As far as I understand, then the teacher is supposed to say, "Yes, you may." Then the student finds his or her seat.

I have asked some of my students about this practice. It is a practice that dates back to their grade school days. If they come late to class and attempt to sit in their seats without going through this charade, they are chastised and told to return to the hall and knock. It is a well-ingrained tradition. Similarly, if these college students want to go to the bathroom, they must raise their hands and ask for permission.

There are other particularities to which I am trying to adjust. Turning off lights is almost like a religion. I was recently sitting with about a dozen of my students in a seminar. One of the administrators came into class to give me some papers. Without asking, she turned off all the lights in the room, leaving us in almost total darkness. There were windows in the room, but it was dark and cloudy outside.

◆　　　◆　　　◆

The German Population Is Leaving

In contrast to some of the more volatile republics of the former Soviet Union, there has not been a wholesale flight of minority populations from Kazakhstan. There has been, however, one major exception. Hundreds of thousands of Germans (who were "resettled" to Kazakhstan from the Volga region of Russia during World War II) have been repatriated to Germany. Their population reached almost 1 million in Kazakhstan. They have been "visiting" Russia since Catherine the Great's time in the late eighteenth century. Despite the passage of time, they have clung remarkably to their culture and language.

The prospect of leaving Kazakhstan is also on every young Russian's mind. But the reality is that there are few desirable places to go, only Moscow and St. Petersburg. Those cities, however, are overcrowded and suffer from a severe climate. Russian friends have related stories of their friends who have left for Russia, only to return to Kazakhstan, having been disillusioned in Russia. "All they do in Russia is drink," commented one young Russian woman. That is quite a statement coming from someone living in Kazakhstan, where they have had some lessons on drinking. In a country in which selection of almost all goods is limited, the kiosks in Almaty are filled with ten or more varieties of vodka.

Those young Russians that stay need to consider their prospects in a country in which they are a minority. As one Russian who does not intend to leave commented, "Kazakhstan is for Kazakhs."

There are some, but not many, Kazakhs who think of leaving. The possibility of their leaving is more a function of disgust over the economic turmoil and the possibility of seeking a better life in the U.S. I met a Kazakh entrepreneur who boasted that he had a million dollars in the bank and wanted to leave for the U.S.

Korean Population

Unlike the German population in Kazakhstan, the Korean population has nowhere to go. The South Korean government has expressed no interest in "repatriating" the Korean population of the Russian Federation or Kazakhstan.

The Koreans were invited to the Russian Far East at the end of the nineteenth century. In 1939, they were deported en masse to Kazakhstan. According to Yura, my driver, an ethnic Korean, Stalin already foresaw the war with Japan and suspected the Koreans might collaborate. If Yura is right, Stalin was losing his marbles long before the end of his life, because there was no love lost between the Japanese and the Koreans. The Korean population is also somewhat insular. Yura is married to an ethnic Korean woman. Most Koreans do not intermarry with other ethnic groups. Yura does not condemn intermarriage, including Russians and Kazakhs, but it is not "desirable." As he said, "It is better to marry one of your own."

Jewish Holidays

Those attending Jewish High Holy Day services in Almaty need no tickets, even though there is only one synagogue in Almaty and only three in the entire country. The vast majority of the Jewish population in Almaty, which reached as many as 60,000 or more by some estimates, has left for Israel, but not because of the endemic anti-Semitism that has persuaded many Jews of Russia and Ukraine to leave. That raw anti-Semitism rarely reared its ugly head in this Moslem region. Nevertheless, only about 8,000 Jews remain in Almaty.

Like other small ethnic communities, the Jewish population remaining in Kazakhstan freely observes its traditions and explores its ethnic heritage. One of the local newspapers in Almaty ran a pleasant if not informative article about the Jewish New Year. The article was entitled: "Let Everyone Have an Apple with Honey," referring to the Jewish tradition of eating apples with honey to inaugurate a sweet New Year.

The synagogue in Almaty is actually a small two-room house in a less desirable part of town on Tashkent Street. A modest metal sign in Russian on the outside gate identifies the house as a synagogue. The first room is the sanctuary, decorated with pink wallpaper and miniature Israeli flags and posters. The second room is for the few women who come to services. The bathroom is an outhouse around back.

Most of the twenty congregants for the High Holy Day Services were elderly men. They represent the remnants of a community of another era. Many Jews from Ukraine, Moldavia, and Poland were evacuated here during the war. Others came after the war, not able to return to their homes. One of the leaders of the community was born in Bucharest and even learned Hebrew as a child. He found his way to Almaty as a safe haven during World War II. One man still wore his full chest of war medals. Another read his prayer book, which had long since fallen apart with no binding. It was simply wrapped in newspaper. As he prayed, he lifted one page from the pile of pages on the left to the other pile of pages on the right.

One member of the congregation hails from Samarkand in Uzbekistan. Many Jews from Georgia and the Caucasus were exiled to Almaty and they are well-represented in the congregation. I met a man and his grandfather at the synagogue whose family originally came from Persia more than 100 years ago, before settling in Georgia. They then were exiled to Kazakhstan. They are preparing to immigrate to Israel in the next few weeks, as soon as they are able to sell their apartment. They continue to speak a language only spoken by Persian Jews. This community is a strange mix of Jewish cultures, but that should be expected in this city on the Old Silk Road from China.

During the High Holy Days, an Israeli came to Almaty to lead services, enjoying a cordial if not overly friendly relationship with the local community. The Israelis who come here to support the community generally speak no Russian, and, even if they speak Yiddish, only part of the congregation comes from Yiddish-speaking communities. The Israeli prayed in the modern orthodox style, foreign to most of the congregants. (There are other groups that come to Almaty to support those with similar backgrounds, such as the Korean community.)

Outside the synagogue, an elderly man with light hair and crystal blue eyes approached me. Almost with embarrassment, he asked me where I was from. When I told him I was from California, he pulled me aside to tell me how he had been beaten on several occasions because he was a Baptist. He shared that he has clung to his beliefs for more than 40 years, living in fear. He now wanted to leave Kazakhstan with his family. As he told me his story, tears flowed down his cheek. An Israeli who emigrated from Kazakhstan in 1990, and who was back in Almaty visiting his family, interceded and told the man that he would be happy to meet with the man and his family but could not promise anything. With gratitude, the elderly man kissed the Israeli—and then me. I later learned that there is a large community of Baptists from the former Soviet Union in Sacramento. For those trying to immigrate to the U.S., without families already living there, the doors for Baptists have been all but closed.

Other than the synagogue, there are other Jewish activities in Almaty. Some orthodox Jews from throughout the world come to Almaty to pray at the grave of the father of the leader of the Lubavitch community. A contingent of young religious women from Israel helps in the community. There is an Israeli embassy in Almaty, but embassy personnel keep a low profile. There are Israeli products such as juices, various premade soups, and of course Israeli vodka—much weaker than the local variety.

When this republic was part of the Soviet Union, the Jews were forbidden to learn about Jewish culture and religion. Most of the Jews in this Central Asian republic have now left for Israel, but the small Jewish community remaining is once again exploring its heritage. Even as their numbers have dwindled, those who have chosen to stay have started a school and cultural center. The Sunday school attracts 120 children from the ages of 6 to 18. As the head of the school told me, "We don't know anything, but we will teach our children anyway."

A Jewish Cultural Day

I learned that the major attraction for the Jewish community is not the synagogue, but Jewish cultural days, which periodically celebrate the Jewish holidays. These celebrations are for the vast majority of Jewish people who don't go to the synagogue. The festivities were held at the "AKhBK Cultural Palace," named after the Alma-Ata Cotton Combine. Constructed in 1981, the Cultural Palace has a modernistic, forbidding exterior. It reaches about five stories high and its auditorium seats 900 people. Approximately 500 people attended the festivities for the Jewish holidays. Considering that there are only a few thousand Jews left in the entire country, the turnout for this extravaganza was excellent. The backdrop to the stage displayed the new Kazakhstan flag, which boasts an ornate design showing a gold sun and eagle in the middle against a background of blue. Draped next to the Kazakhstan flag was the flag of Israel with the Star of David.

The women in Almaty, Russian and Kazakh alike, generally dress very well. Unfortunately, that cultural heritage has not worn off on the Jewish population. The very energetic master of ceremonies was a woman, probably about 30, who was wearing a green and brown vertically striped blouse with a red plaid skirt. Maybe she was making a new fashion statement, but what about the old ladies with their various colored hairdos? They would humble even the most die-hard punk rockers. Punk rockers spend days trying to get their hair color right. These old ladies, with apparently little effort, have been able to bring out deep oranges and purples in their hair. They probably were the role models for punk rockers.

Then we had the entertainment, and, like most amateur entertainment shows, there were some excellent performances and others for which the audience may have preferred to see someone with a long hook to lead the performers off the stage. I sat next to a man who had come to Almaty in 1942, when he was five and an orphan. A childless family adopted him and tried, as he put it, "to make me more Russian than the Tsar." He described his adoptive parents as strident anti-Semites. But he never forgot his heritage. It was strange that, with all the forces compelling him to be Russian, he still maintained his Jewish heritage.

◆　　◆　　◆

A Lesson in Kazakhstan Demographics...from a Demographer

Makash Tatimov is a government demographer with a passion for his work. His office is "decorated" with charts. One of the most interesting is that percentage of Kazakhs to non-Kazakhs (mostly Russians) in the population. In the middle of the nineteenth century, the Kazakhs comprised more than 90 percent of the population, and, even as late as the turn of the twentieth century, Kazakhs comprised more than 80 percent of the population. Tatimov describes this period as a period of "colonization." As more Russians moved and settled the steppe, the Kazakh percentage of the population declined. The major loss of the percentage of Kazakhs, however, did not occur due to colonization, but rather as a result of forced collectivization in 1931 through 1933, when 2.2 million Kazakhs, 52 percent of the Kazakh population, perished as a result of hunger and hunger-related diseases.

In 1933, the Kazakh population became a minority in their own land, comprising less than 40 percent of the overall population. Before and during World War II, whole communities within the Soviet Union were dumped into Kazakhstan, most notably the Korean population from the Far East, the German population from the Volga, and the Greek population. During the 1950s, there was another large influx of Russians. By 1960, the Kazakh population dropped to 29 percent of the entire population. Tatimov and many other Kazakhs liken the disintegration of the core population to the scorched history of the Native American population in the U.S.

Demographic trends again shifted, and, since 1986, the Kazakhs once again comprise a plurality of those living in Kazakhstan. As of 1993, the population consists of 46 percent Kazakhs and 35 percent Russians.

The exigencies of Soviet rule, not the least of which was forced collectivization, scattered millions of Kazakhs across the border. Today, some 3.7 million Kazakhs, or one-third of the overall Kazakh population, live outside of Kazakhstan. More than 1.5 million live in the northwest provinces of China. Some 750,000 live in the Russian Federation. Very few Kazakhs have returned, according to Tatimov. Small trickles of 50,000–70,000 return to Kazakhstan annually.

Almost as many Russians from Russia immigrate to Kazakhstan. In the latest official data, 175,000 Russians have left Kazakhstan in 1993. But according to Tatimov, 70,000 Russians came to Kazakhstan during the same period. The Russian community is much older than the population at large. The average age in the Russian community is 45 years old; in the Kazakh community, it is only 25 years old.

Tatimov estimates that, according to the combined effect of birth and death rates and migration patterns, by the year 2000, Kazakhs will become a majority of the population. According to Tatimov's analysis, 52 percent of the population will be Kazakh and 33 percent will be Russian. Although there are other ethnic communities in Kazakhstan,

Tatimov says that the prospect for ethnic stability rests solely on the relations between the Russian and Kazakh communities.

◆   ◆   ◆

Entertainment—Kazakhstan Style

Almaty grows dark and quiet at night. Few people have money to spend, and the increased street crime is a strong deterrent to those who want just to walk the streets. Even if there were any place to go, the transportation system is inadequate at best to take one to the event. The only big boom in evening entertainment is the casino scene. Unofficially, there are 32 casinos, but only a few major ones. Many of my better students are dealers at the casinos, earning three or four times what their teachers make.

There are only a few decent restaurants, some of which are not very expensive. I can have a good meal for less than $6 at the Shenyang, a Chinese restaurant, but only if I resist the temptation to order frogs. Frogs are not one of the staples of the diet in Almaty, and, as I found out when I took some friends out to dinner, they are very expensive. The locals do not know where most restaurants are because they rarely have the occasion to go out for dinner. For them, the restaurants are of a different world, the world of foreigners, because they are well beyond the means of most people.

For young folks, there are a few discotheques, but the only one where foreigners go is at the Kazakhstan Institute of Management, Economics and Prognostication, better known as Dr. Bang's Institute, which was formerly the Higher Party School. Reservations are required. The discotheque at Bang's Institute is a staid affair. The local young men and women dress to the hilt. Generally, women dress very well in this country; men do not. The foreigners look like they just got off the plane. People don't dance in pairs; they dance in circles and gyrate around the dance floor.

The major entertainment is home entertainment: the television. Every family has at least one television. No one seems particularly deterred from watching television by the crude Russian voice-overs of English language movies or programs. It's amazing anyone can understand what's going on. I recently enjoyed one "free" translation. In English, the man says to a young woman: "You're not wearing your brace." The woman wore a brace on her leg. The voice-over in Russian came out as: "You're not wearing your bra." I rolled over in laughter.

◆   ◆   ◆

Speaking of Transportation

Transportation is a major problem in Almaty. Most people walk or use public transportation, mostly trolley buses and tramways.

Tram coming down the street.

I have not yet experienced public transportation, favoring the system of taxicabs. A program on local television indicated that the city is about 200 buses short, meaning that the buses are overcrowded. Sardines have business-class leg room by comparison. Some of the buses are so overloaded, and the suspension is so completely shot, that they appear about to keel over. Some probably have. The buses and tramways do not follow any particular schedule.

Crowd waits at a bus stop.

Despite the economic hardships, the city is filled with BMWs, Mercedes, and Toyotas. Some of the Japanese models have the steering wheel on the right side of the car. A white stretch limousine has appeared on the streets. When the average salary is no more than $50 a month, one realizes that some people are making a lot more money than the rest.

Gas prices are about 30–35 cents per liter, or roughly $1.20–$1.40 per gallon, incredibly expensive by the standards of this country, but comparable to U.S. prices. Most Kazakhstanis are amazed to hear that their prices are not higher than our prices in the U.S. and that prices in Europe are much higher still. Government gas stations, at which the prices are about one-half the price at other gas stations, command long lines. People can sit days in their cars waiting for gas.

Most of the drivers are young men. If driving a car is any indication of power, then women are without power in this country. I have been here for more than a month, and in that month I have not seen even one woman driving.

The Etiquette of Taxicabs

I can get almost anywhere in town by taxi for about $1, and no more than $2. They are not official taxicabs. They are gypsy cabs, private cabs, or illegal cabs, depending on how you want to characterize them. The procedure is to extend your arm, fingers pointed towards the pavement. If a driver is going in the general direction, he will stop. There is no meter, of course. There are several methods to negotiate a price.

The first, what I call the Moscow model, is to negotiate a price before the driver takes you anywhere. That is the prevalent model followed in Moscow.

The next model is "I'm at Your Mercy." After the driver takes you to your destination, you ask the driver how much the fare is. The driver can think of virtually any amount. Unless the amount is ridiculously high, you are bound to pay the fare.

Then there is the "Is That Enough?" model. After the driver agrees to take you to your destination, you begin to perspire, contemplating what you believe is a fair price. When you reach your destination, you think of the appropriate fare and ask: "Is that enough?" If the amount is in the ballpark, the driver will generally agree. But this model leaves some room for further negotiation.

Finally, there is the "Hand It Over and Run Like Hell" model. Under this model, you still sweat as you contemplate a fair price. But you better have exact change and be accurate. There is no communication. As you are leaving the cab, you hand the driver some money and take off. If the amount is low, the driver might grumble a bit. But if the amount is pitiful, the driver will start yelling after you. Although I have experimented with each model of payment, I have progressed to the "Hand It Over and Run Like Hell" model.

◆   ◆   ◆

A Hard Day at Work—at the Bania

The city celebrated the first ever Almaty Day in the crisp autumn air. The leaves are changing, and the city delighted in the celebration. Strangely, the celebration was similar to the last Revolution Day celebration observed in the final days of the Soviet Union in 1991, except there were no Soviet soldiers this time. The country is obviously making progress: in 1991, at the last Revolution Day celebration, there was only one hot air balloon; for this celebration, there were three.

I walked around the city with Anatoli Didenko, one of the founders of the Private Law College, where I teach my course on U.S. law. Didenko is also the head of the Civil Law Department of Kazakhstan State University. Didenko is a gregarious man, a teacher's teacher. He has labored in anonymity in a neglected area of the law, civil law. Civil law now has become of primary importance in building the legal infrastructure of the country and in attracting foreign investment. Didenko is one of the few experts in the entire country who has a firm grounding in the area. He has become one of the obligatory stops on the Almaty tour for Western lawyers.

Didenko was born in Ukraine, but his family settled in Kazakhstan, in Dzhambul, when Didenko was nine. Didenko studied in Kazakhstan and St. Petersburg. Didenko is an eloquent man with a command of not only law, but also literature. He has written many books, including an excellent exposition on Shakespeare and the law. He is in his late forties and is now teaching his second generation of lawyers in Kazakhstan. He has been offered positions in Ukraine and Russia but has decided to stay in Kazakhstan, his adopted home in which there are few that can match his knowledge of civil law, and even fewer that can match his affability.

We went to the Parliament Building, where Didenko introduced me to Aitbai Konysbayev, a people's deputy who serves on the Committee on Economic Reform. We went to a "buffet," a self-service snack bar at the Alma-Ata Hotel. The hour was early for lunch, so we started right in with the drinking; Didenko and I started with champagne and Konysbayev with vodka. We eventually got around to eating. We sat out on a balcony of the Alma-Ata Hotel, overlooking the festivities below. We analyzed the various difficulties in the country, not the least of which is the ruble zone. Konysbayev was against it, even though he was just in Moscow at the signing ceremony for Kazakhstan to join the ruble zone.

Parliament building on Old Square.

After the alcohol began to facilitate the conversation, we shifted to the difficulties in Moscow. Konysbayev was strongly against the use of force: "You can't achieve a clean end with dirty hands." Didenko was not so sure and, to press his point, recited *Hamlet* (in Russian of course.) We also discussed the prospects of new elections. Konysbayev is keenly interested in the new law on elections. The parliament appears to be grappling with measures to assure a majority of seats for Kazakhs in the new parliament.

After a few hours of sitting on a balcony overlooking the city, we were ready for some genuine relaxation. We went to the Central Market, which is now very clean after the cholera scare. We bought some more champagne and beer and went to Arasan, the magnificent public baths that serve almost 2,500 people a day.

There are three different kinds of baths at Arasan: Eastern, Russian, and Finnish. The Russian bath is very humid. Those partaking of the Russian baths buy bunches of birch leaves, for flagellation of course. The Finnish bath has dry steam. The Eastern bath is a huge room with marble floors. At the outside perimeter, there are alcoves. You eventually work yourself into the center where it becomes hotter. You lie on the warm marble floor with a towel and just relax and let your mind wander. Men and women have separate facilities. We chose the Eastern bath.

Woman selling birch leaves outside the Arasan.

The traditional Russian bania is a way of life here, as in many parts of the former Soviet Union. Many go to the baths as often as once a week. Going to the bania is an art form. You rotate between the sauna and a small pool. When you get a good sweat up and the heat becomes unbearable, you leave the sauna and jump into the small pool, which has very cold water. Then you come out to eat and drink. The process usually takes two or more hours. It is a way of life, a way of bonding, of sharing views without inhibition. It is, of course, a man's domain. The women have their turn, but there is no mixing, except for married couples. The bania is a heritage from Russia, and now it is as much a part of the soul of this country.

Konysbayev and Didenko asked whether we have similar baths in the U.S. I shared with my friends that we had baths in San Francisco, but they were a hotbed of homosexual activity and were closed down with the problems associated with AIDS. They were somewhat revolted and told me that none of the men in the baths here would even harbor such an idea.

We stayed in the baths for two hours, taking a couple of short breaks to drink and to eat our dried fruit and nuts. The deputy's son picked us up to drive us home. We stopped by my house first—but before we arrived, we of course stopped to pick up some more champagne.

"Jewish" Restaurant in Almaty

One of the best kept secrets in Almaty is Shalom, a Jewish restaurant in name only. I had the telephone number of the restaurant and called to obtain directions. Following the directions, I found myself on Panfilov Street and, although I knew I was close to the restaurant, I could not seem to find it. I asked a kiosk vendor where the Shalom restaurant was. "This is the first time I've heard of it," he replied. I eventually found the restaurant along a driveway behind the Alma-Ata Hotel. The restaurant turned out to be 150 feet away from the kiosk where I had asked for directions. The Shalom is a small restaurant and a dinner with alcohol costs more than $25 per person, very expensive by Almaty standards. It is not surprising that the kiosk vendor had not heard of the Shalom.

I tried the Shalom for lunch. The restaurant serves off a fixed menu, mostly Kazakh and Russian food. The waitress told me to come back in the evening if I wanted to try some Jewish food, although she didn't tell me what Jewish food they serve: matzo balls or pastrami and mustard on rye? Doubtful.

The restaurant is very small, just six tables. There is Hebrew lettering on the door, and in the restaurant there is a massive gold and brown Jewish star hanging from the ceiling parallel to the floor. The Jewish star must be six feet long. The decor is "varied." The mirrors and wallpaper look to my uneducated eye like a bordello in the South in the U.S. A ball with little mirrors on it (yes, like the one you saw at 1970s discotheques) swings from the ceiling, casting little green and red circles of light over the room. The Shalom is a uniquely Almaty experience, but not necessarily for those searching for the Jewish spirit of the city.

◆　　◆　　◆

A Housewarming Party

I thought it was time to have a party, bring together East and West (I am not sure which is which). Natasha, my landlord, thought it would not be difficult to pull together. So I invited about twenty people. I knew, of course, that I would commit some faux pas even before I started. I did not plan on serving meat. I planned the event for the middle of the week on Wednesday so that people would not have a day to recover from their hangovers. I informed my guests in advance that it would be an informal gathering and suggested that they not wear suits or ties. I didn't want everyone to stand all night, so I provided seating for my guests.

Then there were aspects of local culture for which I planned: lots of drink and lots of food. I was told that most people planning a party estimate about one bottle(!) of distilled spirits for every two men. Women (and Californians) drink champagne or wine.

Unfortunately, when the woman whom I had hired to prepare the meal (including shopping and serving) fell ill with the flu on the morning of the event, Natasha drafted some friends to help out.

Despite my warnings to my guests not to wear suits or ties, I was the only one in attendance, except the women, who was not wearing a tie. Consistent with local custom, the evening became a formal occasion. The dean of the Private Law College, Anatoli Matiukhin, was the talmada, the master of ceremonies, for the evening. Matiukhin has labored tirelessly to establish the law school, and he is the quintessential dean: gregarious, smart, and engaging.

As host, I had to defer to Matiukhin and could not propose a toast until the end of the evening—when my toast signals that it is time for everyone to leave. The talmada introduces the next person to give a toast. Toasts can linger on for 5 to 10 minutes—all extemporaneous speeches, usually offering tribute to those present.

Matiukhin asked me a little about some of the others present, and then he would extemporize for the introduction. Virtually all of the toasts struck a political chord. Since there were mostly lawyers present, the evening assumed a "legal" tenor, not unlike evenings dominated by lawyers in the U.S. On this night, the small American contingent had long since left, more or less sober, by the time of my toast.

If my gathering had been a traditional Kazakh affair, the Kazakh hosts would have prepared *beshbarmak*, a heavy stew of noodles and chunks of boiled mutton (sometimes horse meat). Before the main dish is served, the sheep's head is offered to the guest of honor as the climax to the festivities. The guest of honor cuts off an ear and ceremoniously passes it to the youngest person so that he or she will listen to wise elders. The guest of honor receives one of the sheep's eyes. I decided to forego the beshbarmak for my gathering.

◆   ◆   ◆

In Need of Interpreters

The Supreme Soviet went into session this week. Nazarbayev opened the session. As the camera surveyed the room, I noticed a strange thing: probably 80 percent of the deputies were wearing headphones for the translation. Nazarbayev was speaking in Kazakh. Even most of the Kazakh deputies do not know Kazakh well enough to listen to a speech in Kazakh without a translation. I know that a committee is working on a law on elections and trying mightily to figure out an effective way to disenfranchise non-Kazakhs, not entirely, but enough to make sure that Kazakhs stay firmly in control of the Kazakhstani government.

The new draft law on the principals of foreign investment would require all official documents to be in both Russian and Kazakh. Those who have worked with English and Russian documents know the huge problems of trying to get translations of documents. What Kazakhstan will do with this power is not quite clear. With Nazarbayev at the helm over the next few years, the political environment should remain stable, but beyond that it is unclear. Kazakhstan could settle into a pattern like Switzerland, where power and influence are held by the Swiss German-speaking population. French-speaking Swiss are quietly resentful of the Swiss German-speaking population, but no one expects armed revolt. The restrained Swiss model would be a good result in Kazakhstan.

The Ruble Zone Comes to Life...and Dies

President Nazarbayev has been a major proponent of tying the monetary policy of Kazakhstan to that of the Russian Federation. The Supreme Soviet of Kazakhstan ratified the agreement to become part of the ruble zone of the "new type" despite considerable opposition in the press. Even after negotiation of the treaty, Moscow made some unreasonable demands, including requiring all gold reserves of Kazakhstan to be transferred to Moscow. Almaty will not accede for obvious reasons, and a new currency will be born. For those waiting with bated breath for removal of another remnant of the former Soviet Union, the day may be near.

3

A New Currency Is Born

November 1993

U.S. Ambassador Comes to Class

The U.S. Embassy is small, but well managed by the U.S. ambassador, William Courtney. Courtney opened the U.S. Embassy in Almaty in February 1992 as Charge d'Affaires and has served as U.S. ambassador since August 1992. He has a PhD in economics and, before the final curtain on the Soviet Union, Courtney served as chairman of the U.S. delegation to the U.S.-Soviet Working Group on Nuclear Weapons Safety, Security, and Dismantlement. His background in economics and nuclear disarmament made him a natural for ambassador to Kazakhstan.

U.S. Ambassador with
Secretary of State Warren Christopher
at U.S. Embassy.

U.S. Ambassador gives lecture at
Private Law College.

Courtney is a straight-shooting professional diplomat held in high esteem not only by American visitors and Kazakhstani government officials, but also by the local populace. Ambassador Courtney is known around the Embassy as a workaholic and has taken almost no time off since he assumed his duties as ambassador. His candor may have something to do with the fact that he hails from Barboursville, a small town in West Virginia. I have discussed with the ambassador my teaching responsibilities and invited him to visit my class at the Private Law College. He readily accepted.

The founders of the school and senior faculty were there to greet him. I introduced the ambassador to my class of about 110 students plus the many visitors. The ambassador speaks Russian very well, and he immediately developed a good rapport with the students. I helped field questions, but I was somewhat dumbfounded by a question about the economic blockade of Cuba. I thought the interrogator was talking about the current situation in Haiti. No, he was asking about the economic blockade of Castro's Cuba.

Then there was a question about Vietnam and U.S. interference in Somalia. I thought it strange that, even for these students in their early twenties, the remnants of Soviet thinking weighed heavily on their lives. They were good questions, but questions I would have expected 10 years ago. The ambassador deftly fielded the questions. There was good coverage of the visit in the national media.

A Visit with the Minister of Justice

The Minister of Justice, Nagashibai Shaikenov, invited me in for a brief chat. He is a young man who was an academic in Yekaterinburg, formerly Sverdlovsk, in the Russian Federation. He has been on the job for only a few months. It was clear that he has already met stiff resistance to some of his plans to reform the judicial system in the country. He also emphasized just how bad the translators are in this emerging country. He took out one of his business cards, produced on poor quality paper, and asked whether there were any mistakes. I counted only three obvious mistakes, not the least of which was "Minister of Yustice."

◆   ◆   ◆

The Holiday That Is Still with Us

There were no military parades on November 7, the day on which the Soviet Union used to celebrate Revolution Day, the holiday commemorating the October Revolution of 1917. Indeed, there was not even a hint in Almaty of the celebrations of the Soviet years with their grand Revolution Day parades. But a newspaper published the results of a survey under the headline, "The Holiday That Is Still with Us." According to the poll, 70 percent of those questioned in Almaty still feel the holiday spirit; 52 percent still consider the day an important day in the history of the country. More than 60 percent of those over 50 still positively evaluate the significance of the October Revolution.

The effect of the October Revolution on the Kazakh people remains the subject of heated debate among historians. Although there was isolated resistance to the policies of the tsar, for 180 years the Kazakhs enjoyed the protection of the Russian empire.

The Kazakhs were exempt from military service as war broke out with the Ottoman Empire and Germany. The pressures of the war prompted the Russian government to implement conscription of Kazakhs in 1916. Some Kazakhs rebelled, but the Russians suppressed the rebellion. The new momentum towards an independent policy for Kazakhs endured.

In the wake of the February Revolution in 1917, some Kazakhs attacked Russians and other Slavs on the territory of Kazakhstan. But the Kazakhs generally greeted the February Revolution with enthusiasm and hope for national territorial autonomy. The Bolshevik Revolution, in sharp contrast, did not command support among the Kazakhs. The Revolution left a void many political groups tried to fill. The two predominant strains of political thought were whether to seek political independence or whether to advance cultural and political autonomy under a confederation with Russia. The debate in Kazakhstan today regarding Kazakhstan's relationship with Russia sounds a strikingly familiar chord.

The former head of the Communist Party of Kazakhstan, Kunaev, gives the official Soviet take on the events of 1917. In his book on Soviet Kazakhstan, Kunaev describes the October Revolution with glowing admiration: "A glorious and very bright page was turned in the centuries-long history of the Kazakh people." The October Revolution became the origin of the "brotherly union of people for the formation of a new society, free from oppression."

Kunaev conveniently overlooks the challenge of the new Kazakh government, the Alash-Orda, which emerged in 1917 as the level of popular content remained high. The policies of the Alash-Orda were strikingly democratic, including separation of church and state; a system of free education; and freedom of speech, press, and assembly. The

central executive body consisted of Kazakh and non-Kazakh representatives. The government came into formal existence in January 1918.
Within a few months, the Alash-Orda decided to cooperate closely
with the Cossacks to defeat their common enemy, the Bolsheviks.
Although this marriage of convenience initially thwarted the Bolsheviks, the military fortunes of the alliance turned in late 1919, as the
Bolsheviks ceased control of most of Kazakhstan.

Although the Bolsheviks originally sought the cooperation of the
Alash-Orda leaders, Soviet historians describe the movement from a
little different point of view: "[One] should not minimize the danger
for the Kazakh people, who came from the Alash-Orda. At first, behind
the obvious demagogic screen, the uneducated and deceived masses of
the Kazakh population could not immediately recognize the true goals
of the Alash-Orda, which, skillfully hidden by a 'national flag,' led it
astray. Alash-Orda was a serious opponent of the Bolsheviks of the
country. In response to the counterrevolutionary armed forces, the
actions of the united forces, the Bolsheviks of Kazakhstan rallied the
masses under the slogans of defending the achievements of the revolution, completely exposing the antipopulist essence of the Alash-
Orda....

"The liquidation of the Alash-Orda was not an accidental phenomenon, but a natural result of its anti-Soviet activity."

The first experiment of Kazakh autonomy was short-lived, but it
represented the first tentative steps towards democratic rule, which
would lie dormant for the next seven decades.

◆   ◆   ◆

An American Friend Comes to Town—and Finally Makes It Past Passport Control

I invited a friend to visit Almaty and be a guest lecturer in some of my
classes. The surprising thing was that he accepted. David is a trial attor-
ney specializing in professional malpractice and personal injury. After

obtaining a jury verdict for his client, he packed his bags for this far away place. Even though he was armed with my past missives from Almaty, David could not be prepared for this extraordinary place. David's visit was like manna from heaven. He brought cassettes, hot cereal, hot chocolate, and Peet's French roast coffee.

The Lufthansa flight always arrives in the darkness at 5:20 in the morning. For those who have visas, it is possible to gather one's luggage, proceed through the bleak terminal, and go through passport control and customs within an hour. I did not have any experience for those arriving without visas. All I had heard was that the authorities would not send those visitors arriving in Almaty without a visa back on the next plane. We had arranged a special invitation for David, and Perzada, the woman from the inviting organization, came with me to meet David. I had forewarned David that whatever takes an hour in the West will take a day here. I don't know whether he believed me—until he was initiated at the airport.

Those with visas were let through. We caught a glimpse of David, who looked energetic, considering he had been traveling directly from California for almost 30 hours. We had to wait outside in the cold. There was only a pair of double-glass doors separating us. David was so close but yet so far. We passed the official invitation to him through the doors, and then we waited and waited.

The visa bureaucrat had to match the official invitation with his own paperwork and then would issue a three-day visa. The pile of papers was in no apparent order, requiring the bureaucrat to sift through the pile for each visa hopeful. David calculated that it took about 30–40 minutes per person. I had to go teach my class at the Management Academy and left Perzada in charge of monitoring David's progress. Perzada continued to stand outside in the cold. It had been warm the day before, but David brought the freezing temperatures back to Almaty. The driver returned, but David had made little progress. Perzada heard that it might be the middle of the afternoon before they released David. She could wait no longer and left.

After classes, I learned that Perzada had left the airport, but without David. I went back to the airport at 11:30 AM, about six hours after David had landed. David was nowhere to be found, and there was no one else left in the terminal from the Lufthansa flight.

Knowing that the airport is not known for its civility, I intently scanned the streets and other terminals. I did not remember whether I had told David the name of the hotel at which I had made reservations.

Finally, at about 1:00 PM I gave up and went home. There were still no messages from David. I started calling the hotel where he was supposed to have checked in and then other hotels, but there was no trace of David. How would I explain his disappearance to his wife and five-year-old daughter? Was it too early to call the police?

At 3:30 I called the hotel again and learned that David had arrived at the hotel. David had cleared the first hurdle of his trip: getting through passport control.

◆   ◆   ◆

Swearing off Drinking

Anatoli Didenko, my colleague at the Law College, invited David and me to Chembulak, the local ski resort. David and I had spent an evening in the bania with other friends the night before and had just a minor amount of booze, compared to what was to come.

Anatoli had prevailed for a client in a housing dispute, and his client Volodia and another colleague, Bakhit, invited Anatoli to celebrate the victory with them at the ski resort. Anatoli used David's visit as a good reason to make the sojourn.

We started to make our way up towards the mountains on Lenin Prospekt. Trees and hedges obscured the old Party haunts on each side of the road. We passed the house in which Leon Trotsky lived in 1928, after he had already been expelled from the Communist Party and before he was forced to leave the Soviet Union. We ascended the steep incline past Medeo, the winter sports stadium. There was no reason to stop at Medeo, the world class ice rink, because it was not yet open. The opening has been delayed because of a lack of Freon.

Medeo.

The road was icy, the Zhiguli was old, and the tires were worn. Let's do this in the summer, I thought. We slid and skidded around the curves. Fortunately, there was a small barrier separating us from the cliff, but I braced for the worst. Volodia works at Chembulak, so I had at least some confidence that we might make it.

We made the first leg of the journey to the dam overlooking Medeo. The Soviets built the dam, commencing construction in 1964 and completing the first stage of the dam in 1972. The second stage of the dam was completed in 1980. The dam rises almost 500 feet from the valley below. Even though the dam is 10 miles from the city, it protects the city from the force of floods from the Malaia Almatinka River. Before the dam was built, torrents of water, mud, and rock would stream down from the mountains, wreaking havoc on the city. Huge boulders in the city are evidence of the destructive power of these floods.

We made it to the top of the dam at 11:00 AM. It was still snowing lightly. As we looked out over Medeo from the dam, our hosts brought out some chicken and salami and, of course, some cognac. I feigned consumption, actually only taking a sip, but I held the glass to my lips a long time. David had been forewarned, but, to be sociable, he quickly downed two shots. I thought this was going to be a long day for David. But he had received my missives from Almaty. He must have known what was coming.

The road beyond the dam to Chembulak was even worse. The director of Chembulak came by in his Neva, a Soviet jeep, and offered to carry the food and take Volodia and Bakhit so they could prepare the table. The Zhiguli did not make it. We parked it along the side of the road and walked the last two and a half kilometers, up a steep windy road that had not been plowed. Only half way through it, Anatoli confessed he had been in the hospital for three weeks earlier in the year with heart problems. Something, I thought, was going to happen—but it wasn't to Anatoli. The drink and time differential would soon take their toll on David.

It took about one and a half hours to get to Chembulak. It was a tiring walk, but the views were magnificent. Although there was snow on the ground, the chair lift had not started operating yet. The table was filled with eats—salads, meats, chickens—and lots of beer, cognac, and other drinks. David did a magnificent job of trying to say no, but he could not fend off the waves of local hospitality brought to bear on this innocent American victim. Bakhit, a woman of good proportion, downed more booze than I have seen of any other woman. She kept on turning to David, saying that, if she, a woman, could drink, David would deal her an insult if he were not to polish off another shot. The booze began to take its effect on David.

The food was another cultural novelty for David; indeed, it was a mystery. At one point, David turned to me and asked what kind of meat had been so elegantly displayed on the table. Please don't tell him, please don't tell him, I thought. There was no reason to increase the cultural gap. Didenko sometimes exercised his English on David, but most of the time relied on me for translation. Did Anatoli hear the question, understand the question? I tried to ignore the question. Anatoli heard and understood and proudly told him, "That's from a horse." David turned a little pale, glanced at me sternly, and said in elegant English, "Keith, I will get you for this." (I guess this means that I won't be having more visitors to Kazakhstan any time soon.) Bakhit chimed in (in Russian) that horse meat was a delicacy. Horse meat sausage, known as *kazi* in Kazakhstan, is a local culinary treat.

After several hours of intense festivity, David passed out in the other room, probably wishing he had never come to Kazakhstan. The original plan was to walk back in the dark to the car. Fortunately, we found a ride in a jeep and dropped David off first. I understand that David made an intimate inspection of his bathroom and, at the risk of insulting our hosts, has sworn off any more liquor.

Black Beauty Revisited

For those who are squeamish, you may want to skip this entry. I went with David to the Central Market today. I wanted to show him how civilized the scene at the Central Market was. The Central Market is very clean and compares favorably to markets in the West. It's not Safeway, but then again it's not the bazaar in Cairo. Prices are generally higher at the Central Market than at other stores throughout Almaty, but products are aplenty, and there is at least a minimal level of supervision for those who can't afford to pay off the food inspectors.

Ethnic Korean women selling salads at the Central Market.

David and I were walking away from the throngs at the Market on a pedestrian walkway. Heading towards us was an older man with a fishnet bag. I knew I shouldn't look twice, but I glanced at the brown furry ears protruding from the top of the bag. No, I said to myself, it can't be. So I had to look again, the kind of morbid curiosity that compels one to look for the injured at the site of an accident. I looked again as the man passed. The blood was still bright red where the horse's head had been severed from the rest of its body. This bag was not headed for the deli at Safeway.

Time to Venture Out and Get a Haircut

The head of a local Jewish organization asked me to appear with him on a new Kazakhstani television program. I readily agreed. The name of the show was something to the effect of "Let's Get Acquainted." The purpose of the show is to introduce the community to various minority populations.

My invitation to participate in the television show prompted me to get a haircut. I would not have waited for one and a half hours had it not been for the urgency of getting a haircut. I needed a haircut. Besides which, this was an entertaining waiting room.

An engineering professor at one of the institutes was engaged in an enlivened debate with another elderly man. The professor was well groomed, although he needed a haircut like the rest of us. He declared that he has been in Kazakhstan for 53 years and has taught for 42 years. He sauntered around the room and tried to engage anyone who would debate him. The young man next to me informed me that the engineering professor had been his teacher. The professor was eminently quotable. "My wife is a doctor. People's immune systems are down. This year, there will be an epidemic of unparalleled proportion." "Life is boring for the youth of today. They're only interested in booze and girls." He also predicted a famine this year worse than in the 1930s. He would make a great radio personality.

Another young fellow next to me whispered, "Doesn't this guy ever shut up?" and was openly relieved when the professor went in for his haircut. I was entertained, and the long wait did not bother me.

The room where the stylists cut hair was just as entertaining. On first blush, the salon looked like any salon in the U.S., but this facade was deceiving. As in the U.S., the stylist washes her clients' hair to make it easier to work with. In the U.S., the stylist gently guides clients into the chairs and backs them up into the basins. During the shampoo, she is very careful not to get any shampoo in their faces or to get their faces wet. The procedure in Kazakhstan is similar, with one minor exception. The stylist guides the clients' heads into the basins, but here it is face first! The shampooing does not last very long; otherwise, the clients would drown as the water pours over their eyes, noses, and mouths. Fortunately, the drain remains open.

I was not altogether displeased by the haircut, and the price was reasonable. It cost about $1 in local currency. The hair stylist was surprised that I gave her a huge tip, another 75 cents.

Central Planning Agency Still Around

After the haircut, I needed to pick up some information at the Ministry of the Economy. I knew the general location but could not find the Ministry. I wandered into the Ministry of Water Resources for directions. An old man still wearing his World War II metals was sitting by the door. His ostensible purpose is to make sure no one gets into the building without the appropriate documents. But he actually fills no real purpose, because everyone who wants to get in goes past him. Even if he wanted to, he would not be able to stop anyone.

I thought at least he could help with directions, so I asked him where the Ministry of the Economy was located. He exclaimed, "Never heard of it. Why don't you ask over at Gosplan across the street?" Gosplan was the central planning agency in Soviet times. I should have known. I went over to "Gosplan," which is now the Ministry of the Economy!

Live on Kazakhstani Television

The evening of my appearance on Kazakhstan television, I had dinner with some of the staff at the U.S. Embassy before I departed for the ominous looking building behind the Presidential Palace: the television station. The building was virtually deserted, except for the team working on the program on which I was supposed to appear.

During the live broadcast, the interviewer gave me a kind introduction as a lawyer and professor at the Management Academy and the Private Law College. She asked me for my assessment of the Jewish community of Almaty. I started to reply that I had been to the synagogue in Almaty, when she abruptly interrupted me and turned to the camera, explaining that she had forgotten to tell her viewers that—by nationality—I was Jewish. I knew I had to correct her without sounding too condescending. I explained that in the U.S., we did not make distinctions based on "nationality." I was an American and also a member of the Jewish faith.

I gave a generally positive assessment of Jewish culture in Kazakhstan. Jewish life is making a resurgence, even though there are few Jews left in Kazakhstan. The virulent anti-Semitism in other parts of the Soviet Union never reared its ugly head in Kazakhstan. Kazakhstan has the potential of becoming a multiethnic haven.

A Ride in an Ambulance

My friend David's ordeal ended. He will not soon forget the ten days he spent in Kazakhstan. He almost did not make it to the plane. I arranged with my driver, Yura, to pick me up at 4:15 AM so we could take David to the airport. Yura arrived on time. It was pouring rain, flooding the streets. I got into the Soviet-make car, a Zhiguli. Yura tried starting the car, but there was no response. Like most drivers, Yura carries spare parts in the trunk. In a driving rain, Yura opened the hood and changed several parts, but all to no avail. Finally, I suggested that we try to jump start the car. For those readers who enjoy the miseries that others suffer, please read on.

David was at the hotel, already waiting in the lobby, so I was unable to call to get a message to him. (For those who think I could call the receptionist to look for David in the lobby, my response is this: "Be real, this is Kazakhstan!") Yura and I were pushing the car down the street in the pouring rain. I was drenched through and through. The street lights were off, so it was completely dark. The car almost engaged a couple of times but didn't quite make it, like so many other machines of Soviet vintage; we deposited the car at the side of the road.

I returned to my apartment to call a cab. They don't have Yellow Cab here. I tried several numbers. The line was either busy or there was no answer. There was only one choice: try to flag down a car on the street. It was just about 5 AM and still dark, and the streets were devoid of any movement. Even the drunks had hunkered down for the night. A lone vehicle came into view as it labored down the street, and thankfully it pulled over. It was an ambulance. The driver wanted to make a few extra rubles, which have become known as "wooden money." Having spent all my rubles, I asked Yura for a few rubles, just enough to get me to the center of town.

I got into the ambulance. Well, I admit I had the heebie-jeebies, especially when I smelled a pungent odor from the back of the ambulance. I was tempted to ask the driver whether we were alone but resisted and left my curiosity unsatisfied. Ignorance is bliss, and for all I knew the next stop for the driver was the morgue. I did not even want to broach the subject. I thought about trying to arrange for the ambulance to take David to the airport. I was indeed sleep deprived even to contemplate the possibility. I let the driver drop me off at David's hotel.

No Longer Walking the Streets in Anonymity

David still needed to catch a cab to the airport, so I asked the woman behind the desk whether she could call a cab. Even though she tried to hide her gray hair with orange dye, the woman behind the desk appeared to be in her sixties. She explained that taxis would not come to the hotel, and in any event the wait would be an hour. She was polite but firmly refused to assist David in getting transportation to the airport. After explaining in detail how she could not help, she broke out into a broad smile, seemingly inconsistent with her statement that she could offer no assistance. She displayed a huge golden smile (read, real gold—there was not a tooth that was not gold capped). Strange, I thought. "I saw you on television the other night. I really enjoyed the show," she told me. "Thank you," I replied, knowing that my stardom was not going to get David to the airport. Fortunately, there were other hotel guests on the way to the airport, and David caught a ride with one of them.

This experience was the first time ever that a stranger had confessed to seeing me on television. I always thought that stardom would have some advantages. Little did I know that the only thrill associated with my 30 minutes in the limelight (actually more like three minutes) would be having an older lady with orange hair and a golden grin pick me out at 5:00 in the morning.

I still had to get home. Same problem: virtually no cars were on the streets. I stood on the street for five minutes before a car passed, going in the opposite direction. He stopped, opened the door, and inquired, "What currency are you paying in?" "Not in your currency," I replied. "Let's go." That was the first cab ride in which I paid in dollars since I arrived.

◆   ◆   ◆

Not the Currency Question Again

The issue of the currency has been an enduring topic. Last weekend, the rumors swirling around the introduction of a new currency became even more persistent. The ruble dropped from about 3,000 to 6,000 rubles to the dollar in a matter of a couple of days. The value of the salary I received on a Friday was halved by Monday.

The value of the ruble took a roller coaster ride that far surpassed the Cyclone at Magic Mountain. Within days, the value had dropped even further to 12,000, but if you were not sick to your stomach yet, within hours pulled back to 7,000. Prices, however, did not keep pace.

It was strange that crowds did not amass at stores at the beginning of the week to buy anything and everything on the shelves. And the prices did not reflect the gyrations in the value of the ruble. A bottle of champagne which cost 15,000 rubles a week ago went up only to 25,000, but, to keep pace with the declining value of the ruble, it should have at least doubled. The purchasing power of my dollar shot up. I am sure that some made hoards of money within a couple of days, and some lost their shirts.

I would have closed down if I owned a shop, trying to minimize the risk and uncertainty. By week's end, only about half of the shops were closed. And although some complained about empty shelves, there were lots of products on the shelves even late in the week. The rumors were fast and furious.

Getting Rid of Rubles in a Hurry

I haven't quite figured out the psychology of lines in this country. I did what I thought made economic sense. When I received my salary, I went out and bought a down jacket of probable Chinese origin. It was not my size, not a good color, and I'm allergic to the down. After I started wearing it, I sneezed all afternoon and somehow in the process lost one of my gloves. I will probably never wear the jacket, but I got rid of a lot of rubles!! I followed the maxim that you had better make sure you buy what you see, because it won't be there tomorrow.

Long Live the Tenge

There was an enlivened and frenetic environment as the city learned of the demise of the Soviet ruble. Long live the tenge, the new currency of Kazakhstan! Kazakhstan will introduce its own currency on Monday at 8:00 AM. On Saturday night, the prime minister went on the tube, excoriating the Russians for forcing Kazakhstan out of the ruble zone. After signing the agreement on the creation of the new ruble zone, the Russians demanded a payment of more than $500 million for the privilege of joining the ruble zone and about $1 billion in gold and other property to be delivered to the Russians. Under the new arrangement proposed by the Russians, Kazakhstan would not introduce its own currency for at least five years.

The Russians have developed a persistent pattern of trying to extract new concessions after an agreement is signed. The Kazakhstanis are tired of being the Russians' lap dog, and now they will remove one of the final formal vestiges of the Soviet empire.

Tensions Run High

I asked many local residents why there were no lines during the time leading up to the introduction of the new currency. "It's just not in our culture," was the general response. And indeed with all the trials and tribulations, Kazakhstanis remain generally calm and collected. This morning, however, this genteel facade began to wear thin. I went out in the elements to buy some bread, and for the first time there were more than 150 people, mostly elderly, in line for bread (the price of bread and other staples would be fixed again under the new economic plan). I decided to do without.

I went by a pharmacy that had not yet opened. A line of 20 formed outside, and I could hear someone testing the glass doors. I went into a market. In front of the dairy counter, an elderly man apparently tried cutting in front of the line. An old lady yelled at him at the top of her lungs. I left before any bloodshed. Even in my part of the city, a generally quiet neighborhood, the streets were buzzing with activity. A car accident heightened the tensions as the drivers decided not to wait for a court to determine who had the right of way.

Kazakhstanis will be able to exchange 100,000 rubles for the new currency at the rate of 500 rubles to the tenge. That's about all of $10–$15, or the equivalent of about 13 large bottles of pickles, which was about the only thing I saw on the shelves this afternoon.

Ethnic Russians in Kazakhstan were interviewed on television and expressed their deep concern about the new currency. They are not familiar with the economic intricacies for and against the new currency. Their concern is much more basic. The ethnic Russian community has close ties with their relatives and friends in Russia. In the Soviet era, travel to Russia was inexpensive. Many studied (and expect their children to study) in Moscow and St. Petersburg. In this part of the world, families are a key source of financial support: children provide financial support to parents, parents to children, and siblings to each other. But now the Russian Federation and Kazakhstan have different currencies; neither the ruble nor the tenge is convertible. The concern of the Russian community in Kazakhstan is that the introduction of a new currency creates yet another layer of difficulties in maintaining their relationships with family and friends.

◆   ◆   ◆

The Challenges of a Hungry American

The first week of the new currency passed without any riots on the streets, a minor miracle. The prices were completely out of whack, and I was still trying to figure out what was going on. The prime minister reported that there was $700 million dollars backing up this currency, which was just enough to build one factory.

The new currency appeared on Monday, the first ever national currency for Kazakhstan. There was a last desperate attempt to buy things on Sunday. I asked an old lady on the street corner how much for a bottle of champagne—"If you're not going to buy it, why ask?" I found another woman who would tell me the price: the price of a bottle of champagne skyrocketed to 100,000 rubles. But one could still eat at the old Communist Party hotel, the Dostyk, for rubles. The price of dinner: the equivalent of 50 cents.

Kazakhstanis were allowed to exchange only 100,000 rubles, and all denominations more than 500 rubles were no longer legal tender after Monday. On Thursday, even the smaller denominations became worthless. Uzbekistan unveiled its new currency on the same day, and now Moldova and Belarus are debating whether to unveil their respective national currencies.

The Law College called on Sunday and the Management Academy on Monday to find out whether I would exchange any currency. I spent all of my old Soviet rubles the previous Friday, thinking that I had "beaten" the system. When I learned that I could exchange 100,000 rubles for 200 tenge, roughly about $50, I was disappointed that I had not played the game right. Then I had to stand in line on Monday to exchange dollars for tenge. I went to the Dostyk Hotel, the most exclusive hotel in town, which has an exchange office. Just as I arrived, the exchange office ran out of tenge, but the clerk promised to open later in the afternoon.

I returned later in the afternoon and saw that a line of about twenty hearty souls had formed to wait for tenge. As I waited, a waitress from the restaurant upstairs had given me some money to exchange so she would not have to wait in line. I waited for one and half hours and almost reached the front. I could feel the new bills touching my fingers. Hooray! I would have the new Kazakhstani currency. But it was not to be. The exchange office ran out of money with only one more person to serve before me.

The major problem for the week was how to eat. I had only a short supply of food, but I went through most of what I had over the weekend. Hard currency restaurants stopped accepting dollars. "Ruble" restaurants would not take dollars, only accepting small ruble bills or tenge. I had neither. I hadn't eaten lunch, and now dinner was passing through my fingers. Although the director of the restaurant sternly told prospective patrons (most of whom did not understand a word of what she was saying) that she would not serve them, the waitress whom I had agreed to exchange money for agreed to seat me. I had lunch and dinner—and paid for it. The waiter gladly took my dollars, eleven of them, at the same place where the day before I could have eaten for 50 cents. I could not finish my last dish, but, not being bashful or, more accurately, being desperate to have a supply of food for the following day, I took out a plastic bag, and spooned the food into my makeshift doggy bag. I felt no shame. I was just a hungry American.

The Bob Berg Quartet came to town in the midst of the chaos. The group was here as "cultural ambassadors" on a U.S. Information Agency program. As I was eating my dinner, Bob Berg walked in the restaurant. From what I could surmise, he was accustomed to luxury and did not like this adventure. He was less than enamored of the chaos, especially when he and his fellow musicians could not get dinner because they did not have tenge. I told the group's American escort just to sit down and order and worry about paying later. Were they really going to make the Quartet wash dishes for their meals? Not likely.

Lines for bread have appeared throughout the city. I still have not bought any bread for two weeks. Being a spoiled American, I don't have the stamina to stand in line for tasteless bread. (In the Soviet era, bread was delicious. There was a time, in the early 1990s, that a company exported fresh bread from Moscow to New York. That seems like a long time ago. There are three major types of bread—two of which I find completely tasteless and the third of which is rarely available.) I am hopeful that this will be the week I manage to buy some bread.

On Monday, the exchange office at the hotel gave 4.7 tenge to the dollar. On Tuesday, only 4 tenge. Did the tenge strengthen in 24 hours? No, the distribution network was so poor that there was a huge shortfall in the circulation of tenge. If others were like me, they would have paid anything for the tenge, just to eat. On Tuesday, a bank president interviewed on television boasted that the new exchange rate was fair, because foreigners were standing in line at his bank to exchange dollars for tenge. Was it confidence in the tenge, or just some very hungry Americans?

On Tuesday, I stood in line for another 45 minutes. The rate was four tenge for the dollar, but I could only exchange $10. If I could eat at restaurants and buy food at comparable prices as before the exchange, a few dollars would carry me through a few days. But the hard currency restaurants doubled and some even tripled their prices. The Italian restaurant at which I could eat two weeks ago for less than $2 cost $7 this past week for a coke and spaghetti. The prices in dollars and tenge had gone out of sight. Snickers bars cost three tenge on Wednesday and five tenge by the end of the week.

There were some hard currency restaurants and stores still open this week, but the next day was D-day. All hard currency operations were to be closed down. Even the black market was not yet working. A friend went down to buy dollars, but without any luck. There was a

100-tenge fine for illegal exchanges, a huge amount of money for those living on a standard local salary.

At the week's end, the rate was maintained at four tenge to the dollar. The purchase price for dollars was six tenge to the dollar. Even after a week, at least half of the shops were still closed. Russian currency was particularly valuable. I went to the market. Prices were especially high, and probably 70 percent of the usual vendors were not working, thinking that it was better not to work than to earn tenge. Others were hoarding products. The kiosks were slowly reopening, but very slowly. Prices were very high, maybe reflecting the true value of the tenge.

◆   ◆   ◆

The Lawyers' Conference

The Minister of Justice invited me to a conference for Kazakhstani lawyers at the Ministry of Justice. Invitations were strictly limited, as there were fewer than 300 seats in the auditorium. Many lawyers had resisted the meeting, knowing that a reform package would be introduced. Over the days leading up to the meeting, some lawyers gathered behind closed doors to attempt to derail the conference. When the conference was convened, everyone expected some drama. They were not disappointed. As if to underscore the importance of the conference, President Nazarbayev sat at the dais alongside the Minister of Justice.

Kairbek Suleimenov presided over the conference, identifying two main purposes of the conference: to debate a legal reform package and to establish a national bar association. Minister of Justice Shaikenov introduced his legal reform plan. He initially discussed the need to reform legal education within the country. He is a strong proponent of a bar examination and the need to close down most of the for-profit law schools that have recently opened in the country.

Shaikenov identified the obvious: there is a severe lack of legal specialists in the country. Many of the qualified teachers have gone into politics or into business; and some, like one preeminent expert in criminal procedure, have left for Russia. Shaikenov also discussed the need for a new procedure for legislation. The problem is that new legislation is passed sometimes by way of decree from the president's office, sometimes from the legislature. And draft laws sometimes are mysteriously changed at the last minute. Laws are passed and some are not published; even when they are published, they are published in only one of several general circulation newspapers. Shaikenov proposed a new Institute of Legislation under the Ministry of Justice to write and coordinate legislation.

In one of the more controversial components of his legislative reform package, Shaikenov proposed to unify the two court systems, the commercial courts, which hear disputes between enterprises, and the courts of general jurisdiction, which hear all other disputes. Trying to protect their territory, the commercial judges are strongly against this part of the package. Shaikenov also supports the formation of a new bar association. He also wants to institute a bar examination, a judicial exam, lifetime appointments for judges, and funding from the republican budget for courts to bolster the independence of the judiciary.

Judge Tomas Aidmikhalibetov, the head of the Supreme Court, sounded out against Shaikenov. He agreed that legal reform was necessary, but he condescended towards Shaikenov: "You are new here. You are young. We have been working on legal reform since 1988." Aidmikhalibetov likened the conference to a gathering of mice, during which the mice discuss how to protect themselves against a cat. All they need to do is to hang a bell on the cat to warn against the cat. All the mice agree, but then the question arises of who will hang the bell on the cat in the first place.

Aidmikhalibetov was particularly against the appointment of judges by the president, referring to the American experience in which a majority of the states hold elections for judges. Nazarbayev, who hadn't spoken a word all morning, interrupted Aidmikhalibetov: "Only in two states," Nazarbayev corrected him. Nazarbayev was wrong, but that nuance was lost on the audience. With those few words, Nazarbayev made it clear that Shaikenov had already garnered the support of the president. Aidmikhalibetov was left to speak out for an increase in the salary of judges.

There was a line of other speakers who discussed the various aspects of the program. One jurist spoke out forcefully against the introduction of juries, because they were too expensive. Then the drama began to unfold. Suleimenov gave the floor to Sultan Sartaev, the head of the Union of Lawyers. The Minister of Justice had refused to reregister the Union, causing Sartaev great consternation. Sartaev was ready with a feisty speech, accusing the president of abandoning him. Sartaev argued that the president had assisted Sartaev in establishing the Union. Sartaev had brought significant international delegations to the country, presenting them to the president. He had arranged international conferences. Sartaev waved in his hand the charter documents of the Union, in Russian, Kazakh, and even English. "The Minister of Justice had no right to refuse to register the Union," Sartaev argued. Nazarbayev interrupted Sartaev, "O.K., but what about your views on the need for legal reform?" With those few words, Nazarbayev had stopped Sartaev dead in his tracks. It was clear what path Nazarbayev would take.

Some of the speakers used Western practice as a significant point of departure, even though many of them knew of Western practice only from books. The distinguished jurist, Salik Zeimanov, spoke out eloquently in favor of legal reform, quoting Thomas Jefferson. The Supreme Court had become a little Ministry of Justice, according to Zeimanov. An independent judiciary was critical to the evolution of Kazakhstan.

Nazarbayev finally got his chance. He first addressed the introduction of the new currency. "All of the difficulty is still ahead," said Nazarbayev. He talked about the need for "our own policy," to get out of the crisis. "We can't just print money. People need to work for tenge.

He recognized that monetary policy was not popular, but he said, "Forget about me. What will happen to the state?"

Nazarbayev then discussed the need for legal reform, but distinguishing the experience of other countries. "We haven't lived with 250 years of democracy. We're not American or French. We're Russian, Kazakh, German, and so forth." He then cast his unwavering support for Shaikenov. "No one says that he is deficient in his knowledge of the law of the Soviet Union or Kazakhstan." He then implored the audience, "Support him!" The main task before the country is "how to build the state structures of this young country."

He saved the harshest criticism for Sartaev. "I respect him," said Nazarbayev without looking at Sartaev, who was sitting right behind me. "But he hasn't done anything." The velvet dagger had found its mark. The audience was dead silent. Nazarbayev suggested that the only reason for the creation of the Union of Lawyers was to select a deputy in parliament, when certain social organizations, rather than the people, were empowered to select deputies. As head of the Union of Lawyers, Sartaev had spent most of his time abroad, advancing his own personal agenda.

Nazarbayev then hinted that the Constitution would soon need to be amended, even though it was only adopted earlier this year in 1993. According to Nazarbayev, the Constitution was a transitional document. The Constitution discourages economic development. For example, he pointed out that the right to housing may be inconsistent with privatization of housing. Also, "we now have freedom, but how does that freedom affect others?"

He also spoke of electoral reform. Nazarbayev wants to appoint 42 deputies himself. The electorate would elect 150 deputies from separate electoral districts. I almost gasped as I heard this clearly undemocratic proposal.

Nazarbayev wanted to dissolve the local soviets. He pointed out that, if there were heated discourse in the local soviets, such as the debate he witnessed at the Lawyer's Conference, a head of the local soviet would "throw a bucket" at the dissenting member. The heads of the local soviets have cars and status, but they have no function. The local councils are "dead entities," according to Nazarbayev.

The audience had remained uncommonly quiet during the lengthy speech. Nazarbayev concluded his speech with the following pronouncement: "There is only one path: that is forward." Nazarbayev's command of the audience was absolute.

The following day I met with an exhausted Shaikenov. I congratulated him on his victory. He was clearly elated, as he should have been, because any reform in this country is the political equivalent of changing the direction of a tanker: it happens slowly and is fraught with danger.

4

No More Parliament to Kick Around

December 1993

Local Soviets Dissolved

We have had a cold winter. The temperature dropped to around 0 degrees Fahrenheit, 5–10 degrees colder than Moscow. There has been snow on the ground for weeks. I learned that my Russian hat I bought in Moscow in 1977 would no longer do. As my driver told me, "don't worry about leaving it anywhere. No one will steal it."

Despite the cold weather, the political climate heated up, keeping pace with the fast-moving events in Moscow. The political intrigue captivated the attention of the capital. At the Lawyer's Conference, President Nazarbayev blasted local soviets as holdovers of the Soviet era. Within days after the conference, the local soviets were closed down. Doors were locked, and officials were not allowed in their offices. The legal basis for the dissolution of the local soviets was not clear. No one was able to tell me under whose authority the local soviets were shut down. Nonetheless, the local soviets went quietly. There was virtually no resistance.

New Elections—but There Is No Election Law

Election fever gripped Russia as it prepared for national parliamentary elections on December 12, 1993. Now, in turn, it is time for Kazakhstan to try its hand at elections. The presidium of the Supreme Soviet met with Nazarbayev. The parliamentary session scheduled to open later this month will likely be the last session for the Supreme Soviet. In a display of the post-Soviet brand of demagoguery, the president wants, and will likely get, new elections as soon as March 1994. But he wants to do it the Kazakhstani way, not the "Moscow way," meaning tanks, dead bodies, and the like.

Foreign investors were waiting expectantly for new laws on concessions, oil and gas, foreign investments, but they will have to be patient. The Supreme Soviet has other things on its agenda. It is a lame duck parliament. For the next several months, governmental power will be centralized in the presidency. Instead of too much government, there will be no government other than presidential decrees.

The Election Code—Is This Democracy?

According to one deputy with whom I spoke about the new election code, the major challenge facing drafters is how to maintain a substantial Kazakh majority in parliament, while implementing a democratic electoral system. About 75 percent of the current parliament is Kazakh, but only 45 percent of the population is Kazakh. If the electorate voted along ethnic lines, the Kazakh representation in the new parliament would represent not even a majority. In the U.S., each party would try to gerrymander the electoral districts, but not here. Forget about legal niceties such as gerrymandering or language requirements. The Kazakhstani solution is much cruder. Under the guise of needing a "professional" parliament, Nazarbayev wants to appoint, or as he calls it nominate, about 25 percent of the seats in a new parliament.

The new election code is probably the singularly most important piece of legislation for this country. And it highlights that even a modicum of democracy will be hard to come by in the new Kazakhstan. It is no wonder that most of the young Russians I meet are contemplating leaving.

◆   ◆   ◆

Language Barriers Pose Problems

The new currency exacerbated the daily living challenges, especially how to eat. Since the introduction of the new currency, the only decent meal I had was for Thanksgiving. I shared Thanksgiving with some folks from the embassy, who had a turkey flown in from Frankfurt. Our Thanksgiving was probably not exactly what the pilgrims envisioned in 1621. Unfortunately, Thanksgiving only comes once a year.

Since Thanksgiving, I have had no choice but to venture out to the few hard currency stores to buy some food, but these stores posed a different set of challenges. I was prepared to make myself a great dinner last night: spaghetti, tomato paste, mushrooms, fresh bread…Mmm! One problem: I bought the "tomato paste" in a hard currency store, at least it looked like tomato paste, as far as a can looks like much of anything. I opened the can and found miniature corn. I went back to reexamine the can. It showed miniature corn with tomato sauce on top. The label was in German, of which I do not even know one word. The label was advertising the corn, not the sauce. Do you know how pasta and miniature corn tastes with ketchup for flavoring? It will not rank as one of the mistaken great discoveries of the culinary world.

I tried again to prepare another package of food, but the directions were in Italian. I thought I understood everything except one word, *mezzo*. I was supposed to add *in mezzo litro di acqua*. As I looked at my creation, it occurred to me that *mezzo* may mean "half." So my rice and mushroom dish looked more like rice and mushroom soup, or just rice and mushroom mush. The foreign community at least has a fighting chance to eat. But it is not easy unless you can read Italian.

Shopping for meat at local market.

Social Life Comes Alive

I attended a friend's birthday party this past week. Birthdays are big in Kazakhstan. There is very little else to do, so people celebrate their birthdays in style. People save their money for months to throw a good party, which includes copious amounts of music, food, and drink. Although most birthday parties are held in the home, this party was held in a restaurant to accommodate the large number of family and friends. There were about 80 people around this huge table in a separate hall. We were lucky there was a good turnout, because the hall was very cold, and we needed one another for warmth.

Between the toasts, the crowd danced, not with anyone in particular, just gyrating to the music out in the middle of the floor. A good portion of the male crowd retired to the corridor for a smoke. In accordance with the tradition in this part of the world, guests gave some gifts, and many just gave cash donations to the honoree. They came up to the guest of honor, gave him a big kiss, and slipped him some cash.

I met some local judges and thought that I had found some soul mates. One of the judges may have been the only person in the room not drinking. In the former Soviet Union, the only convincing and polite excuse not to drink is being the one "behind the wheel," i.e., driving. Any other feigned excuse is an insult. But when I probed the judge, he came up with a novel reason for not drinking: doctor's orders. He was suffering from a liver ailment.

◆　　◆　　◆

Cognac with a Cossack

Earlier this week, I spent the entire day in student conferences at the Law College. Meanwhile, the faculty and staff at the College were in the administrative offices upstairs, celebrating the one-year anniversary of the College. They encouraged me to imbibe some of the plentiful booze. But I had a good excuse. I needed to be sober for my students. I agreed that, if my students did not make it to any of the meetings, I would be glad to return and partake. The last students did not make it to their meetings, leaving me no choice other than to make the lonely trip up the stairs to the offices where the festivities continued. I knew what my fate would be. But when I arrived, much to my delight, most of the booze was already gone, or so I thought.

Ziia Atashevich Mukashev is a professor of philosophy. He teaches at the Law College. The young students present wholly different challenges than Mukashev's students at his previous school, the Higher Party School, which trained students for work in the Communist Party. Mukashev sports a gray beard without a mustache, accentuating his round face. He speaks eloquently, but his language is difficult to comprehend at times. Nevertheless, there was no mistake when he insisted that I fulfill my promise to drink. I glanced at the empty bottles on the table and told him that I would if there were any drink left. I had grossly miscalculated. This wily man in his late sixties was prepared. He reached in his brief case and pulled out a shiny metal canister filled with cognac. The door was closed and there was no escape.

After a few friendly drinks, it was time to return home to prepare for my lecture the next day at the Management Academy. Wrong again…it was time for a night cap. The dean of the Law College, Anatoli Matiukhin, agreed to take Mukashev and me home. (Anybody who has a car has a responsibility to take his friends home, even if they live on the other side of town.) We were supposed to drop Mukashev off at his apartment first. But Mukashev insisted that we come in, just for a few minutes.

As we sat in Mukashev's kitchen drinking cognac and vodka, Mukashev displayed an intimate knowledge of his ancestors. After a few toasts, the words began to flow easily. With pride, Mukashev declared that he was a Cossack. Mukashev was born in 1926 in Almaty. His grandfather was a successful merchant, but during the Revolution the family "lost everything." In 1922, his grandfather died, leaving five children, one of whom was Mukashev's mother. One day at the bazaar, Mukashev's father eyed a beautiful 16-year-old girl. They were married a few months later.

Mukashev's parents settled down in a town several hundred miles from Alma-Ata. Although they prospered, Mukashev's grandparents wanted the family to return to Alma-Ata. The family loaded their belongings into a cart and set out on the two-month return journey to Alma-Ata. The rain was unforgiving. Mukashev's father developed pneumonia, and, soon after the family returned to Alma-Ata, Mukashev's father died.

Mukashev's mother remarried and Mukashev assumed the last name of his step father, a Kazakh. Nevertheless, when he was required to declare his "nationality," he decided to list the nationality of his natural parents, Tatars, even though he recognized that his choice would later mean greater difficulty in entering the university or landing a job in Kazakhstan. The registration of nationality had "colossal significance," recounted Mukashev. If Mukashev were proud of his Tatar roots, why did he tell me he was a Cossack?

Mukashev's great-grandfather lived on the Volga River in Kazan. Kazan was a Tatar stronghold until 1552, when the troops of Ivan the Terrible captured the city. Searching for opportunity, Mukashev's great-grandparents packed their belongings and set out for opportunity in the East. In 1857, they arrived in the Alma-Ata region, in what was then known as Vernyi, a fortress established in 1854 as part of the expansion of the Russian influence into the steppe. Kazakhstan was fully incorporated into the Russian state after the defeat of the Kokand khanate in 1864–1865, and the settlement at Vernyi was rapidly expanding when Mukashev's great-grandparents arrived.

Mukashev's great-grandfather began to prosper as well. He opened a store and sold his wares to Russians and Kazakhs. Since Tatar is a Turkic language similar to Kazakh, Mukashev's father could easily converse with the local Kazakhs and was treated as "one of their own." Mukashev's great-grandparents had three sons, one of whom showed some interest in continuing his father's trade. This was Mukashev's grandfather. He was accepted as a Cossack. But what is a Cossack?

Mukashev had problems with this question. He first told me that the Cossacks were a "military organization" but then referred to the Cossacks as a separate people. He explained that Cossacks trace their roots to Turkic tribes who migrated to the Don River in the fourteenth century. They had a "free-spirited way of life, and did not want any government. They were completely free." But they eventually agreed to serve the tsar on the frontiers of the Russian empire. They spoke Turkish amongst themselves, but they also had a command of Russian. According to Mukashev, they were the "means of the tsar's expansionist policies, especially in Kazakhstan."

The tsar's regular army captured the cities, and then the Cossacks secured the area, establishing settlements. Some of the cities around Almaty were originally Cossack settlements, including the town in which Nazarbayev was born, Chemolgan. The Cossacks were the privileged, the aristocracy. They ran their towns according to a strict hierarchy, at the top of which was the "Ottoman," their elected leader. With the governor of the region in Omsk, almost 1000 miles away, the Semireche Cossacks of Kazakhstan (which included the area around present-day Almaty) lived semiautonomously.

Only Tatars and Russians could become Cossacks. Ukrainians and all others need not have applied. The candidate applied to the Ottoman, who convened an assembly, at which the Cossacks would vote whether to accept the candidate into their ranks. Russian peasants and fugitives and others for whom a free-wheeling existence held some allure enthusiastically joined the Cossacks. Once a Cossack, "there was no nationality." The only important factor was the Cossack's horse, saber, and ability to use weapons. The Cossack's male children also became Cossacks.

Mukashev informed me that the Semireche Cossacks recently elected a new Ottoman. The Cossacks in the north agitated to secede from Kazakhstan. Although he did not endorse this movement, Mukashev could not resist the temptation to muse about the enormous wealth that the Cossacks would have if they were independent. He was aware of the tension between Cossacks and Kazakhs, but on the ethnic question, Mukashev said: "I am absolutely indifferent."

The hour was very late and the booze had exacted its toll. Matiukhin and I left Mukashev, even though Mukashev entreated us to stay longer. I left the preparation for my class until the next morning and continued to contemplate my cognac with a Cossack.

◆   ◆   ◆

Plot Thickens in Parliament

The plot thickened this past week in this country that is trying to find itself. Tulegen Moldabayev, who works on the Legislation Committee in parliament, invited me to the opening session of parliament. Security was tight and drama was heavy in the air. The balcony was packed with press people and other observers wanting to experience the last session of this parliament.

Only a few foreigners were allowed in the visitors' gallery. Ambassador Courtney had received an invitation. Other Embassy staff members were not allowed into the session. The parliament took a couple of procedural votes and then voted to meet in closed session, banning everybody who was not a people's deputy. Those in the visitors' gallery became *persona non grata* and retired to the reception area on the first floor. The ambassador commented, "We are refugees." And of course he was right. Banning the press and visitors from the proceedings was a strange first step to democracy.

We waited in the hallway, where the parliament had set up an elaborate buffet. We were left to speculate about what was going on behind the closed doors. After waiting for a couple of hours, word leaked that the parliament was considering how best to dissolve itself. In the meantime, Nazarbayev summoned Moldabayev for a meeting. I later learned that Nazarbayev appointed Moldabayev to the Central Election Commission.

Later in the day, the proceedings were reopened. The parliament considered a few issues, the most important of which was dissolving itself. All other legislation had to wait until after new elections. The parliament set the elections for March 7, 1994. In the meantime, the president would likely receive extraordinary powers so that "there is no vacuum of power in the interim," according to one deputy who came out to brief the press.

The mayor of Almaty was interviewed on television to explain the rush to elections. The mayor of Almaty was a presidential appointee. Many in this town shook their heads in disbelief that the mayor, Zamanbek Nurkadilov, was appointed by Nazarbayev. Before independence, Nurkadilov was the first secretary of the Communist Party of Kazakhstan for the Alma-Ata region. Nurkadilov is still considered by many as a Party hack, even though appointed by Nazarbayev. Nurkadilov looks the part. Nurkadilov is a rotund man. His neck is so short that his collar seems to disappear under his jowls.

According to Nurkadilov, the new elections would be held in March of 1994, rather than in May, because it was not fair for the people involved in agriculture to take time off to vote in May. Former communists are still not known for their linguistic creativity. The actual reason is that Nazarbayev's slate of candidates is well organized in every single one of the regions. A March date would not allow any serious opposition to materialize.

The parliament was still in session, seeking to resolve a few remaining issues. It then would hang the "OUT OF BUSINESS" sign by the middle of this coming week. Even though one of the purposes of the new parliament was to have a more "professional" parliament with new faces, many of the old faces would be in the "new" parliament.

Zbig Comes to Town

Zbigniew Brzezinski, National Security Adviser in the Carter Administration, was in Almaty on a speaking tour. The U.S. Ambassador hosted a dinner for Brzezinski, inviting a few Americans and some deputies who were still licking their wounds from the parliamentary session earlier in the day.

Brzezinski is still much respected in this part of the world, as many credit Brzezinski for foretelling the fall of the great Soviet empire. The deputy foreign minister and other deputies were eager to schmooze with Brzezinski. Not surprisingly, the hot topic of conversation was the elections. Under the draft law, there would be a single house of parliament, with 177 new members. Of these, 135 would be elected by the people from various districts, which have not yet been defined. A candidate would not need to live in the district to run as the district's representative. As one member told me at the reception: "I will run wherever I think I can get elected."

The president would nominate individuals for the remaining 42 seats. Murat Raev, one of the authors of the election code, gave a preview of the presidential list. The president would name 50 individuals for the presidential list. The new parliament would then select 42 names to seat the new members of parliament.

It may be foreign to our notion of democracy for the executive branch to dictate the membership of the legislative branch. But, according to Raev, this new system would assure that there were competent members of the new legislature. It has become in vogue to parrot the words of President Nazarbayev: Kazakhstan needs a professional parliament. He meant not only a sitting parliament, but also a parliament comprised of professionals such as economists and lawyers. Under this system, many of our presidents would probably not have been able to seek elective office: Jimmy Carter, a peanut farmer; Ronald Reagan, an actor; and George Bush, an oilman; all would not have had the requisite experience to serve.

Brzezinski answered a few questions from the parliamentarians and other government officials. He suggested that two elements were necessary for interethnic harmony: democracy and prosperity. Kazakhstan would likely prosper, but Kazakhstan was not yet a democracy, according to Brzezinski. Brzezinski shared his views on how to nurture political and economic stability. Kazakhstan, according to Brzezinski, needed a partner. He discounted Russia, China, and the Arab states to the South. "What about Ukraine?" Brzezinski asked rhetorically. Anyone reading the news knows that the Ukrainian economy has been in a free fall. The budget deficit is 70 percent of the GNP! Schools have been letting their kids out because there has been no heating fuel. I thought it was a strange suggestion, except when one considers that Brzezinski has strong ties to Ukraine.

◆   ◆   ◆

St. Moritz It Isn't

I returned to the mountains, the scene of the crime, where Anatoli Didenko brought me and my friend. This time, my intentions were to breathe the mountain air and stay away from the booze. This time, I caught a taxi, a good sturdy car that managed to take me past Medeo and up to the steep grades leading to the dam. I ran into the same problem as on my previous attempt to ascend the mountainous road. The last steep incline is unforgiving, and the driver could not make it up the grade. He let me off to climb the last mile of this hellish grade.

There is a "shuttle service," trucks that were once used to transport Soviet soldiers. But I found out too late. They could not stop to pick me up because they would not be able to stop and then start again up the icy grade. Many cars did not make it and turned around. Other drivers, however, tapped their ingenuity and resourcefulness. With these road conditions, it would be preferable to have front wheel drive cars. So how do you convert your rear wheel drive to front wheel drive? Easy—just go up the hill backwards. So what if it is more than a mile. Several cars made it up the hill this way, turning their cars around, putting them in reverse, and maneuvering up the hill. One can't argue with success!

The trip to Chembulak was worth it. It had been gray and overcast for weeks. A low cloud cover lingered over Almaty, preventing the sun from shining through. Almaty is surrounded by mountains, and the smoggy air hovers over the city. But once you go out of town towards the mountains, it is crystal clear. There are no clouds in the sky, just fresh invigorating air, and a spectacular view of the rugged Alatau Mountains.

The ski "resort" is basic. There are four "lifts." (I put everything in quotes, because I can't bring myself to dignify any of the facilities with equivalent Western terms. That would present the reader with a fundamentally flawed perception of this experience.) The Yugoslavs built the lifts. The "chair lift" is essentially just that, *one* chair, about the size of the seat in a shopping cart, suspended at the end of a bar. As skiers go up the mountain, they feel very exposed. There is a basic metal bar that falls across the midsection, but I wouldn't rely on it. The T-Bar is a palma lift, one person at a time; they don't believe in camaraderie here either; it is a solo experience. There is a 6" disk that is throttled through the legs. For the guys, hopefully there won't be any big bumps on the way up.

Chembulak.

The slopes are intermediate. Since there were few people on the slopes, there were virtually no lines, and few people to bump into. The rental equipment at 100 tenge, about $16, is not bad. And an all-day lift ticket costs 25 tenge, about $4, for the day. My overall assessment: I will go again.

◆   ◆   ◆

Male Embryos—Watch Out, Difficult Economic Times Ahead

One of my neighbors came over to talk. She is a young Russian woman who just turned 21 and, to my eye, not unattractive. Like many young women, she is concerned about the prospects of marriage. Men and women in this part of the world typically marry in their early twenties. She asked whether I knew of any introduction services in the U.S. so she could leave Kazakhstan.

She told me that she was looking for an intelligent man around 25. I inquired whether it was really that difficult to find someone here. She said that she is popular, but "I can't find anyone." She wants to leave because, in Kazakhstan, she feels uncomfortable. And besides which, "I don't like Kazakhs," she candidly confided in me. "In Moscow I feel more at home."

Are you still sitting down? A lonely Russian girl does not make it onto these pages by asking about dating services. Her explanation of her predicament is what draws special comment: "Why look in the U.S.? There must be intelligent, attractive men here or in Russia," I asked. Her stunning reply: "Because there are more men there. It is a well-known fact that there are fewer men here." She elaborated: "Male embryos fare worse in difficult times. Baby boys are less adaptable and many die." My eyes widened. "There are fewer men to choose from both here and in Russia," she concluded.

The Soviets lost a generation of men during the World War II and in Stalin's labor camps, but succeeding generations have not been similarly handicapped. Nevertheless, there has been this persistent misconception that there are many more women than men of all ages in this part of the world. It is strange how a 21-year-old woman still clings to this notion.

Young Russians Ready to Leave

My neighbor is typical, young and mobile with relatives in Russia. She studies in Moscow and wants to leave Kazakhstan permanently. Here Russians are of a "second sort," she told me. Many young people have shared with me this same outlook. Their parents, on the other hand, seem content to stay. I have met very few young Russians who are not contemplating leaving.

A Russian woman with a young daughter came over to my apartment for some tea recently and could barely contain her wrath at the Kazakh community. In crude language, she spouted her bitterness at what she perceived as the relegation of the Russian community to second-class citizens. With little prompting, she told me how her grade school daughter was taking a class in the Kazakh language when her teacher told her that "this is our country," and that she, the daughter, need not learn Kazakh. She should just leave the country. Although the conversation can not be verified, most certainly the mother has shared the story with her friends, adding to the tension between the Russian and Kazakh communities.

The election in March 1994 could become a watershed for this country. It is still too early to predict whether there will be adequate representation of minority communities. The current parliament is 75 percent Kazakh, even though they constitute only 45 percent of the population. Probably Russians and other non-Kazakhs will make a marginally better showing than the current underrepresentation of their number in parliament, but not sufficient to convince young ethnic Russians to stay in the country.

Russians perceive that their opportunities are severely limited. The best jobs go to Kazakhs. Members of delegations traveling abroad are mostly Kazakh. The universities are Kazakh. A provocative article appeared recently in the national press, which portrayed a bleak picture. According to the article, the official emigration statistics have not been released for months. Those Kazakhs living in other parts of the former Soviet Union have little problem receiving permission to live in Kazakhstan. Ethnic Russians living in Kazakhstan have to endure a long and sometimes unsuccessful process to have their relatives join them in Kazakhstan. International delegations are almost all Kazakh. The article analyzed the disproportionate and pervasive Kazakh influence at every level of government.

I have heard rumors that, in some western towns, the effort to get rid of non-Kazakhs has already begun. Are they only rumors? There is a steady stream of Russians leaving. The government maintains that 175,000 ethnic Russians left in 1993. The newspapers published unofficial reports that the figure was closer to 250,000. That is not a flood, but the trend could easily accelerate. Can Nazarbayev keep a lid on this potentially explosive situation? The election could begin to tell the story of what this country will look like in the coming years.

◆   ◆   ◆

Are Those Tenge—or Rubles?

Some quarters derisively refer to the new currency as Nazarbucks. On the streets, the masses refer to the tenge by another name, the ruble. The actual name just hasn't caught on. When I go into the stores, the salespeople still quote prices to me in rubles. The cabby asks for three rubles. The woman selling bread in the government store asks whether I have 3 kopeks. They are referring of course to tenge and tiyen.

The government is selling precious hard currency reserves to support the tenge—introduced at about 4.7 tenge to the dollar, now at about 5.5 and a market rate of about 6.5–7.0. Despite the support, there are reports that, in some of the northern regions of the country, the market exchange rate is even as much as 17 tenge to the dollar, almost three times what the dollar will bring in Almaty. Indeed, all I know is that I lost about 50 percent of the purchasing value of my dollar overnight. A Western economist in Almaty told me that he expected me to recover, at most, only about 70–80 percent of the purchasing value of the dollar after the tenge floats. For noneconomists, it means this: it has become very expensive to live in Almaty. The government intends to let the tenge float within a few weeks, and then the value of the tenge will drop rapidly.

Fortunately, most of the kiosks and other stores have reopened. Goods have reappeared. The lines which grew rapidly in the period leading up to the exchange and which continued for weeks have now abated. Despite all the uncertainty, the tenge is slowly settling in.

◆　　◆　　◆

And Then Some Days Are Just Hell

I had the flu, and I know exactly how I was infected. When I went to a party recently, a woman sat next to me, whispering sweet niceties into my ear all evening and sneezing all the while. I have tried several interesting home remedies, suggestions from friends. For a cold; try tea, vodka, and jam! For a cough; here's just the remedy: have some strange woman place mustard paper on your chest and back and then cover you up in towels and wait for half an hour until it burns. The home remedies uniformly failed to provide any relief, but then I am not a true believer, which may hinder the effectiveness of the remedy.

I had planned to show a video in my class at the Management Academy. I was sicker than a dog, but there was no way to put the day off. A video should be an easy endeavor for a teacher, right? Not here in Kazakhstan. One might assume that this old institution would have a VCR and a television. Not here. A student picked me up and we went to the Embassy, which had agreed to lend me a VCR and TV. It was snowing and the roads were slick. We made it to the Academy and carried the equipment up five flights of stairs. My assistant was late getting to class. The 50 students in my class were out in the hallway while we waited for my assistant to get the key. Then, of course, the TV had a U.S. style plug that does not go into the wall. After we confirmed that the TV was 220 volts, one of my students somehow rewired the TV and placed live wires into the outlet. Although about an hour late, *it worked.*

The videos were a hit, as students attentively listened to the American programs on business, which had been translated into Russian. In the meantime, I worked with some of my students in another room. When I calculated that the videos were finished, I came back to the classroom, but the students were still sitting there, their attention fixated on the television. Then I glanced at the tube. The videos were indeed over, and the students had turned the channel to the soap opera, *Santa Barbara*.

I had arranged with my driver to pick me up at noon. One of my students helped me carry the VCR and television down five flights and out to the street, where it was still snowing heavily. My driver did not show up. We placed the equipment in my student's car, recognizing that it would be dangerous to leave it there, but not having any strength to carry the equipment back up five flights of stairs. He remained in the car, guarding the equipment. I retired to my office for my student meetings. When I was through, my student drove me back to the Embassy to return the equipment. Sometimes, it's better not to get out of bed.

◆   ◆   ◆

The New Version of the Election Law—or a New Interpretation

Tulegen Moldabayev, who sits on the Central Election Commission, shared with me a new interpretation of the election law. According to this new version, Nazarbayev would nominate candidates to a "governmental list" of parliamentary candidates, who would stand for election by the voters on election day, rather than be seated by the new parliament.

This new interpretation is a major development, not the version of the election law that Nazarbayev announced at the Lawyers' Conference a few weeks earlier. Although this novel model does not comport with democratic principles in the West, it is a much better version than the last iteration of the Election Code. I do not know whether the foreign community who cornered some of the authors on the cocktail circuit had anything to do with the change—but I would like to think that we had some effect.

◆   ◆   ◆

Second Independence Day—More Fun than Revolution Day

The news about the second "Day of the Republic," the Kazakhstani Independence Day, is that it was uneventful. The second Independence Day, observed on December 16, was a very quiet affair—almost no affair, other than a day off of work. Aitbai Konysbayev, a former people's deputy, invited Anatoli Didenko, my colleague from the Law College, to his house for a celebration. Konysbayev was out of a job but did not seem distressed at the prospect of looking for a job. He might run for the next parliament.

In a sharp departure from the Soviet years, there were no military parades. The evening news program carried a message from the U.S. ambassador, congratulating Kazakhstanis on their country's independence. The news also carried clips from a celebration at Panfilov Park. One young boy remarked: "This is even more fun than November 7," the old day to commemorate the October Revolution.

◆   ◆   ◆

A Word about the Darker Side

A news program showed in graphic, gory detail the corpses of two men gunned down in the downtown area, the victims of what looked like a professional hit. One of the victims, I. Milgrom, was the head of a construction company. His driver, D. Tarasov, was the other victim. They were brazenly gunned down on the steps leading to Milgrom's apartment. Almaty is not immune.

Americans have not been the target of this kind of vicious crime. Nevertheless, out of an abundance of caution, the U.S. Embassy called recently, advising me that Salman Rushdie was received in the U.S. I was told to be especially careful in case Iran decided to carry out its death sentence or other mischief on an American surrogate for Rushdie. I was walking with a friend a couple of days later down a quiet street, when he pointed out that we were walking by the Iranian Embassy. So much for precautionary measures.

Armed for Dinner

Several weeks ago, I went back to the Shalom Restaurant. I was enjoying a nice, quiet dinner with a friend when a man walked into the restaurant, escorted by two bodyguards. The two burly bodyguards took off their jackets. The bodyguards looked nothing like Kevin Costner. Under his jacket, one of the men wore a shoulder holster with what appeared to me to be an automatic handgun. The other bodyguard had an Uzi machine gun. The head honcho sat in the corner surrounded by his two bodyguards. Every time the door opened, I looked around to see whether I needed to find cover. Fortunately, they stayed for only about 40 minutes. When they left, the remaining patrons could relax again.

Armed for the Slopes

Last weekend I went skiing. I had struck a barter deal: a ride to the slopes in exchange for a free ski lesson. My intended victim was the first deputy to the ambassador for Turkey. My friend picked me up in his jeep. He brought along his friend, a college-aged American woman. She had not been skiing since the first time she did battle with the slopes and lost, breaking her leg. But that was 12 years earlier, and she was ready to attack the slopes again. Fortunately, the second time on skis was uneventful. By the end of the day, they were both skiing down the bunny slopes, precariously but with some success. But what I did not know…

The young American woman had some aches and pains, and not only from falling on the slope. We went back to the apartment of my friend, the Turkish diplomat. I took a double take, as he pulled a Smith and Wesson handgun from his trousers. He recounted how earlier last year he had encountered some hoodlums outside a hotel. They started to beat him up, until he had a chance to pull his gun from his pocket. The assailants quickly dispersed. Later that day, the Turkish diplomat was attacked again, probably by the same hoodlums, and this time he exercised his right of self-defense. He shot one of them.

He doesn't go anywhere without his S&W, and he doesn't leave it in the car, which brings me to the point of the story. What did he do with his gun while he was on the slopes? His friend, the American woman, had washed her jacket before we went skiing, and so she had to borrow one of his jackets. She chose the warmest one with all the pockets, leaving him with a short jacket. So guess who got the gun? She did, and, when she fell on the slopes, it wasn't always on soft powdery snow.

If I Had Been Armed

The weather was good in the mountains. Cars could actually make it up the steep road. I had to wait in what one could call a sorry imitation of a line. People cut in line from both sides. Some brazenly skied right to the front of the line, took off their skis, jumped the short fence, put their skis on, and grabbed the chair lift. An extra five or ten minutes in line would not have affected me, but, after 45 minutes in line, I began to ponder what I would do if only I were armed.

When I was almost at the front of the line, a local man came up to me and asked, politely and in Russian of course, whether I would mind letting his guests go in front of the line. He explained that they had come all the way from America (and obviously could not wait in line for 45 minutes like the rest of us)! Despite my compliant disposition, I did not let them go ahead. I explained that I too was from America and had waited in line like the rest. Nevertheless, the skiers waiting in line behind me let "our American friends" go ahead. So much for my principled stand.

5

Celebrating the Holidays

January 1994

The Year of the Dog

The Chinese calendar will inaugurate the Year of the Dog this year. The former Soviet Union watches these things very closely. When I was in Moscow in 1990 for the New Year, my hosts presented me with a toy horse. I thought that it must be a Russian tradition to give toy horses for the New Year. It wasn't until the following year, when the same people gave me a toy goat, that I realized that my friends in Moscow were not observing a Russian tradition, but rather honoring the Chinese New Year.

The main holiday in the former Soviet Union is the New Year. No one celebrates "our" Christmas day. There were no Christmas trees or lights on the streets as I strolled down Toli Bi Street on Christmas Eve. There was no trace of the holiday. Few foreigners were left in town. The omnipresent drunks were not celebrating anything in particular. They were just in their normal drunken stupor, completely oblivious to the fact that hundreds of millions of people around the world were celebrating Christmas.

On Christmas Day, my friends all wished me a Merry Christmas. Even when I explained that I did not celebrate the holiday, they said, "Oh, then you must not be a Catholic." They are much more directed at Catholics than Protestants here. But I did have a festive dinner on Christmas, even though no one at the gathering celebrated the day as a holiday. All the guests were Moslem, Russian Orthodox, atheist, or

Jewish. My Russian and Kazakh friends who are aware that Americans generally celebrate Christmas extended their greetings for Christmas. I accepted their greetings.

The Russian Federation and even Ukraine give their workers a day off to observe the Russian Orthodox Christmas on January 7. Most people in Kazakhstan, regardless of ethnic origin, are unaware of that holiday. The day after Christmas, the U.S. ambassador invited the few Americans remaining in town to his apartment for a Christmas celebration. That was my only sense of Christmas.

◆　　◆　　◆

The New Year and a Leg of Lamb

Everyone readies for the New Year for weeks. They buy their New Year's trees, buy presents for friends, and typically celebrate the New Year's with their families at home. I did not look forward to an unending bout with the bottle for the New Years' celebration. I still had the enduring memory of a celebration a few years ago in Moscow, when I dealt my hosts an unforgivable insult when I left the festivities early—at 4:00 AM.

Bob Post, the cultural attaché at the U.S. Embassy, invited me to an outing in the mountains outside of Almaty on the way to Talgar. Before we left, we stopped in at the home of one of the organizers, Malek, who refused to let us leave until we were able to partake of his hospitality: cognac and horse innards. I passed on the horse innards. Bob was not as lucky.

We were supposed to meet our group at the Golden Ear Sanatorium in the mountains. A sanatorium is not a nut house here, but rather a hotel of sorts. The ear does not refer to a part of the human anatomy, or any part of the anatomy of a horse; rather, it refers to the ear of a cereal plant. The group numbered about 40, including several families with children. Most of the adults, who were of various ethnic backgrounds, had known each other since grade school.

This may have been the first time that I spent any time with other Russian-speaking Americans: Bob and another American, Dennis, who works at Deloitte and Touche on a privatization project. The local contingent had a difficult time keeping our names straight. Bob, Dennis, and Keith all sound about the same to the local community. Dennis was called "Bobe" (rhymes with "globe"), I was called Dennis, and Bob was called "Keet." We look nothing alike, but, on the other hand, to some locals, all Americans look alike.

I anxiously waited to see how my fellow countrymen acquitted themselves in the face of entreaties for them to drink. I wanted to see how they balanced the physiological constraints of drinking too much with the cultural imperatives. They are younger than me and were probably much better acquainted with college beer bashes. They responded in the only rational way possible: they retired to their room, hoping that the locals would not find them. I did. When I came into their room, Dennis looked up from his bed, "Oh, I am glad it's an American." I was thrilled to learn that I was not the only American to demur in the face of the drinking challenge.

Without hosts urging the bottle into my hands, I could enjoy myself without the bottle. Only those who have been in this part of the world know how pervasive the bottle is. Did you know that some Russians leave Kazakhstan for Russia only to return with one major complaint: they drink too much in Russia? It did not occur to me so clearly, until I went away with some folks over the New Year's weekend, that everyone here drinks, almost without exception.

We occupied an entire floor. At the requests of our hosts, we had brought our own stereo. I suppose a hallway is a hallway. The scene was probably similar to a Motel 6 somewhere, except for the paint on the walls. The penalty for leaning against the wall: you were marked for the weekend. The paint was more like chalk and, whether in your room or in the halls, it would come off. Everyone was walking around with chalk on their back.

The American contingent brought some good bottles of wine in celebration of the New Year. The Kazakhstanis allowed us to pour it for them, but they hated the stuff. They looked at it, but they could not drink it. We had an excellent bottle of French wine and they couldn't drink it. They will drink and eat anything...except a good bottle of French wine.

The weekend had its highlights. The children put on a skit. We all went into an enormous indoor swimming pool, which was freezing cold. Snow fell all weekend, providing a magical quality to the scenery. According to one of the administrators at the sanatorium, this weekend was the first time that the sanatorium remained open for the New Year. Everyone was trying to figure out ways to eke out an existence.

Back to the party: the unremitting party dragged on for two entire days. The drunken stupor that falls on the heels of drinking one's self into oblivion is a great equalizer: the unintelligible utterances, the rolling eyes, the stumbling around aimlessly. (Am I being a little harsh? Even the fellow who helped establish the first Alcoholics' Anonymous gave me a lift home after a party a few weeks earlier, after having more than a couple of drinks.)

A party is not a party without lamb. The "chieftain" of our hosts invited me to slaughter the lamb on Saturday morning. The not-so-sharp knife was right in front of me. I could see the lamb expectantly waiting for the end. I declined the honor. The chieftain did not appear very skilled, as the lamb seemed to linger between life and death. But the blood stained the fresh snow. I was not as queasy as the first time I saw this ritual during my first visit to Kazakhstan in 1991; but, if you don't like to be in the front row to witness a circumcision, then this lamb slaughtering business is also probably not for you.

That night, it was time for more partying upstairs in our "Motel 6" near Talgar. If I closed my eyes, I could have been anywhere with the loud music, people drinking, dancing. But this was not a scene from Iowa or Illinois. It couldn't be, because there was one telltale sign of local custom. The garbage box was filled to the brim, and, on top of the garbage, there was a leg of lamb with the wool still on it and a tiny hoof, leaving no room for imagination. This was not the leftovers from L'Olivier's Fine Cuisine.

A Shot in the Dark

The final farewell left an indelible imprint on my memories of that weekend. One of the passengers in the jeep on the way home was one of the worst offenders of the weekend. He had started drinking at 8:00 in the morning. He was totally wasted and engaged in lewd, crude, and disgusting repartee, but fortunately I did not understand a good portion of what he said. I had noticed his gun while we were at the sanatorium.

On the way back, our passenger decided to load his gun. Even though he could not see straight, he placed the bullets into the barrel. I may have shown my discomfort. Dennis, sitting next to me in the back seat, had the dubious honor of holding the gun for safekeeping. In the meantime, our passenger boasted that his 6-year-old son had caused a scene in Bishkek a few years back when he shot a gun in the air.

Dennis returned the gun to our local passenger at the end of our short trip. Our friend invited us up for a nightcap. We declined and decided to retire for some hot chocolate at my place. It was a welcome change to the booze. This Kazakhstani bid us farewell, like a mother waving longingly after her children, except that he had a loaded gun in his right hand. The *coup de grace* was his final gesture, unloading a couple of rounds in the air. Like son, like father. I was glad to get home…

◆   ◆   ◆

Back to the Slopes for a Close Call

I was back on the slopes before the New Year. You will recall my friend from the Turkish Embassy and his American friend, both beginners whom I have been trying to teach how to ski. She was doing fine until she did a reverse snow plow. Even the usually insensitive bystanders probably detected something had gone awry when they heard the piercing screams from the American woman, Melanie. No, she was not O.K.

I and several others helped her down the mountain in shifts. My partner was a gap-toothed Kazakh wearing a huge earring through his right ear. We arrived at the doctor's office. A slender young man looking pale, as if all the blood had run out of his body, was sitting on a chair, and some guy who I suppose was the doctor was giving him a huge shot in the shoulder. I thought that Melanie, who was not a happy camper before we got to the "doctor's office," was about to bolt. Forget about the leg.

There was one other problem. There were about five guys hanging around this office, and, of course, for the doctor to view her leg, Melanie would have to undress. I was sure that she was about to bolt. I explained the delicate situation to the doctor. All of the guys except the doctor would leave, and she would get a robe. It was not exactly a robe, but a dirty old blanket covering a sofa. The doctor worked magic. First he put the shoulder of his other patient back into place. It turned out he had a dislocated shoulder. The doctor then felt Melanie's knee and leg through the clothes, determining that nothing was broken. Melanie would not have to undress. That was the best news Melanie received all day.

Remember the Yugo

An article appeared in the local press about Chembulak, the ski resort, likening it to Switzerland. The author has obviously not been to Switzerland! I love Chembulak. It is my major respite from the challenges of living in Almaty. It has fresh air and breathtaking views. It is not, however, Switzerland.

The lifts at Chembulak are of Yugoslav manufacture. I thought that they were of an older vintage, but they are actually only ten years old.

The three palmas and one chair work…sometimes. The cable broke on the palma lift recently, leaving only two barely functioning palmas.

◆   ◆   ◆

Bidding Adieu to the Old Parliament

The old deputies have vacated their old offices. Some are running in the March 1994 elections; some are looking for jobs; and some are just contemplating or mourning the possibilities. Some may argue that the government did them a disservice, luring them into service and then dropping them, or forcing them into oblivion a couple of years before their term expired. Some may have prospects for running in the coming election, but of course over half of them are out of work. Those with no constituency are waiting for the presidential list, which could come out in the next couple of weeks; but, for most, they have had their turn in the political limelight.

The text of the election code finally appeared. There will be one house of parliament, in which 177 deputies will serve, about one-half the size of the former Supreme Soviet. The electorate will choose 135 deputies in various electoral districts throughout the country. Each deputy will represent one of the 135 electoral districts. The other 42 deputies will also be chosen by election. The president will nominate 3 or 4 candidates from each of the 21 administrative units in the country (19 regions and 2 cities). The top two vote-getters will sit in the next parliament. The districts could still easily produce a one-sided ethnic mix in the new parliament; but it appears more likely that there will be "only" a 55–65 percent Kazakh majority in the new parliament.

Dinner with a Composer

I attended a dinner with a composer, Tulegen Mukhamezhanov, who is also active in politics. He unabashedly recounted his Communist Party past with some pride. He was one of the 5 percent of the population who were members. Unlike many former communists, Mukhamezhanov did not try to hide his background or say that, although he was a member of the Party, he "never agreed with it," or "yes, I was a member of the Party, but I was working for change from within."

Mukhamezhanov is from Semipalatinsk. Semipalatinsk is the Nevada of the former Soviet Union, the site of nearly 500 nuclear detonations. Mukhamezhanov recalled the first blast when he was growing up in the 1950s. "The whole earth shook, and there was a spectacular light show," Mukhamezhanov recalled. As a child growing up in Semipalatinsk, Mukhamezhanov saw many of these light shows, never understanding and never being forewarned of the dangers.

Mukhamezhanov, an ethnic Kazakh, spoke openly about his belief that the country should do everything in its power to keep the Russian population from leaving Kazakhstan. He has been to America and understands the power of diversity. I have heard this sentiment from other Kazakhs, but there are few Kazakhs like Mukhamezhanov who would be willing to reinstate Russian as an official state language on a par with Kazakh. Now that would be a powerful message.

Even though about three-fourths of the candidates running for parliamentary seats are Kazakhs, Mukhamezhanov predicts a non-Kazakh majority in the new parliament, believing that the Kazakh candidates will split the vote of their constituents. Russians believe that the districts have been gerrymandered to throw the vast majority of the seats to Kazakhs, as in the old parliament.

Mukhamezhanov even told the following anecdote to illustrate his point. There are three caldrons in hell. In the first, the Jews are boiling for their sins; in the second, the Russians; and in the third, Kazakhs. A guard watches over the Jews to assure they don't escape eternal damnation. The guard for the Russians is asleep. And there is no guard for the Kazakhs. What's the explanation? The devil explains: The Jews help each other, so we need to be vigilant that they don't get out. The Russians are confused about how to get out, so the guard can doze off. The

Kazakhs jump over each other. If one is about ready to get out, the rest will assuredly pull him back. No guard is needed.

The anecdote did not fit the stereotype of Kazakh tradition, in which family and friends are of paramount importance. Kazakh families are reportedly small clans, and each member shares his wealth even with distant relatives.

◆   ◆   ◆

And Now for the Economy...

The tenge is falling like a rock. There is not much faith in the new currency. It was introduced at 4 tenge to the dollar. Within two months, a dollar was selling for 12 on the black market. Fortunately, inflation has not kept pace. The snickerometer (i.e., the cost of the ubiquitous Snicker's bar) shows that the economy is holding steady. The cost of a Snicker's bar today is about the same as it was when the tenge was unveiled two months ago. In general, prices have gone up about 50 percent, but the value of the tenge has dropped almost 70 percent at the free market exchange rate.

A Sample of Market Clearing Prices

The omnipresent traffic cops stand on street corners, closely eyeing traffic. In contrast to their Western counterparts who cruise the motorways, the Kazakhstan traffic cops merely hold up their batons, signaling for drivers to pull over for minor infractions and sometimes even for no apparent reason. Often times, they do not write a ticket, but instead they negotiate a separate price with the driver. If offering a bribe were a serious offense, there would not be any cars on the streets. The prices are well known: 20 tenge for seat belts, 30 for speeding, 40 for running a light, and 200 for drunk driving. These prices do not amount to extravagant sanctions by Western standards, but, in this country, they represent almost a month's salary for some.

Traffic policeman eyeing the road.

Some drivers merely keep a gift at the ready in the car for the traffic cops. A driver recently took me home for free, just because he liked talking to an American. We exchanged telephone numbers. As he reached into his glove compartment, I spotted a bottle of vodka in a sack. "That's for the traffic cop," he exclaimed.

How Much for a Professor?

And of course there are prices for professors. Certain professors have a certain price to "earn" a grade in their course. According to one of my students, one professor at Kazakh State University has been taking four bottles of vodka for twenty or thirty years. At least that way, the professor does not have to deal with the fluctuating value of the currency over the years. Some of my students have told me that the going price is 50 tenge for a pass/not pass course and 100 tenge for a grade. Fortunately, I have not been approached.

The temptation for teachers to accept bribes is great in a country in which academics are paid less than their students. Some of my students who work nights at local casinos earn five times my monthly salary, and I am the highest paid faculty member in my department at the Management Academy—when I get paid. This month, I have not yet been paid at all. The department with which I am affiliated for administrative purposes (different from the department in which I have been teaching) collects the salaries of the teachers. The secretary called to have me pick up the salary, but I could not come down that day. I told her I would pick the salary up by the end of the week. She was worried that someone might steal the money from the safe in the faculty office, so the secretary took my salary home with her. She commutes on the bus, known for its theft problem.

Natural Hazards on the Streets of Almaty

One of the benefits of teaching is that your successful students, who make more money than their teachers, usually stop and drive their teachers wherever they happen to be going. I often walk with Anatoli Didenko, a colleague at the law school, which has been renamed the Higher Law School "Adilet," Kazakh for justice. Didenko has already taught an entire generation of lawyers in Kazakhstan, and, on the strength of his stature, we have received rides from his former students. Even some of my students from the law school have seen me trying to catch a cab. In accordance with tradition, they picked me up to take me to my destination.

Didenko's former students invariably approach Didenko during our walks in town. Recently, one of his former students came up to us in a store. Didenko introduced me as his colleague from the U.S. The former student had just returned from New York and, with great enthusiasm, enumerated the host of problems she witnessed. She must have thought that the streets were paved with gold and was relieved or even joyful to observe some of the problems in the U.S.

Walking on the streets requires a careful attitude. I do not have in mind the criminal element here, or even the risk of encountering former students to whom I gave a failing mark. Even the cars or the manholes without covers present manageable challenges. There is another hazard on the streets. Kazakhstanis, young and old, incessantly spit this way and that. Don't overtake someone on the street walking too closely, and don't walk down wind.

◆   ◆   ◆

The Gettysburg Address in Russian

I completed my teaching responsibilities at both the Management Academy and the Adilet Law School. At the Law School, I concluded my course with a reading of the Gettysburg Address. The Address probably sounded different in Russian. Little did Abraham Lincoln know that his words at Gettysburg would endure not only in the U.S., but also in a far-off land known as Kazakhstan.

My students at both the Management Academy and the Adilet Law School did not expect to work hard in my courses. As one student confided to me, "teachers do not expect us to work, so why should we?" And, indeed, why should they? They take as many as thirteen courses every semester, leaving little time to prepare for class. Students earn their grades based on oral examinations at the end of the semester—except in my courses, in which I implemented a more traditional Western standard. The teachers have every incentive to pass their students; otherwise, they have to administer another examination a few weeks later. The whole thrust of the grading system is to push the students through the program.

In my course at the Adilet Law School, I required of each of my students a paper comparing an aspect of U.S. law with Kazakhstan law. The student was free to select the area of the law. I would have passed any paper showing even a paltry understanding of the two systems. But there was a minor setback. Some students collaborated more than I would have wanted, probably thinking that I would not read any of their papers. They submitted carbon copies, yes, carbon copies, of someone else's paper. The administration did not seem surprised by this phenomenon, and no students were expelled. The offenders received another chance to write another paper.

The materials some of the students used were very old, testimony to the lack of current literature. Here is a quote from one paper I received: "The largest effect of constitutional doctrine is the strengthening of the bourgeoisie domination in forming the state mechanism and facilitating the ruling class' firm control over all facets of the political process." Indeed. Fortunately, of course, the student simply copied the text directly from one of the books in the library. We would have a serious problem if this were his independent thinking.

More puzzling was the following assertion in a paper purportedly on the jury system in the U.S. "On receipt of such a statement [given by witnesses and accusers] and looking for other evidence, the police systematically undertake violence and other unlawful methods of conducting the investigation, and go unpunished for this." Where did he get that information?

Teaching at the Management Academy Draws to a Close

The Management Academy invited me to share my observations about my class with other teachers in the management department. About 25 teachers attended. Before this meeting, I had the feeling that my efforts were for naught or just that I would not see the fruits of my efforts for a long time to come, possibly like my first grade teacher, who may—or may not wonder what happened to me 30 years later.

The head of the department introduced me to my colleagues. He is a man of the "old" school. Even though he is Kazakh, he talks like Brezhnev, slowly and deliberately with a dry sense of humor. I gave my candid views of the term, knowing that it was too late to fire me. The goal of my course was to try to bridge the gap between theory and practice. The students have a fine idea of what business is in theory.

They have books in Russian that convey the idea eloquently, but they still have only a vague notion of what it is to run a business. Their idea of business is barter or trade, known here pejoratively as speculating.

I did not know what I should expect of the students. The students of course expected a "*khaliava*," known in American parlance as a mick, an easy course. With thirteen subjects on their schedule, an easy course would have been a welcome respite for the students. Much to the students' chagrin, this American professor was an exacting taskmaster.

Students formed teams to work on various business plans. The projects included building an ice cream production facility, manufacturing women's clothing for "full" women, and operating a casino. As the semester progressed, many students became increasingly enthusiastic about their projects.

My major administrative challenge was obtaining information. Even obtaining chalk was never easy. Strange as it may seem, even with chalk, some of the chalk boards cannot be written on, unless the teacher wants to write on the board with invisible ink (chalk). I never did see an eraser. My students became the primary source of information. When I commenced the course, the dean told me that the course would go until February. In mid-December, one of my students told me that the last day of lectures was at the end of December.

During the course of the semester, a steady stream of teachers visited my course. After I concluded my presentation, they had their chance to comment on my "method" of teaching. One teacher commented on the fact that I had demanded that students type their papers and that, despite all of the problems of finding typewriters (typewriters were registered with the authorities in the Soviet era), somehow the students found a way to get their papers typed. Another recalled how I required students to come to class on time.

One teacher stood up and decried the administration for spending money on a new marble entryway when the Academy desperately needed money for computers and other equipment. The new entryway is a particularly visible source of irritation because the needs of the Academy are vast, and the ostentatious entryway shows just how out of whack the priorities of the Academy are. For example, the lights in the Academy were recently turned off for several weeks to conserve electricity.

I think that the teachers who visited my course also gained some valuable lessons. I had labored the entire semester under the impression that my presence would have little effect on students or faculty. I am satisfied now that I may have left some meager prints in the sand.

◆　　　◆　　　◆

Burden to Make a Name for Myself: The People of the Blue Planet

Almaty boasts some intriguing people. Alexander Sergeevich Danilov is a man consumed with a passion for collecting information on the notable personalities since the beginning of recorded history. Over the past fifty years, Danilov has collected biographical information on some 250,000 people, all without the assistance of a computer. He has named his project "the People of the Blue Planet."

Danilov was born in 1927. He is of slight build and has a kind but almost nondescript appearance. Although he grew up in Vladivostok in the Soviet Far East, he traveled extensively with his parents. He never left his books far behind. In the sixth grade, he had already collected 787 books in his own personal library, "not including my parents' books," Danilov emphasized. He readily offered to show me the catalogue which he has preserved to this day.

Although he received a medical education and worked at a time as a medical assistant, Danilov decided to forsake the meager existence of the medical field to work in the backbreaking but well-paid coal mines of Southern Siberia, and later in the gold mines near Magadan in the Soviet Far East. After he and his wife were able to retire, they needed to decide where to settle on their pension. Not surprisingly, they wanted a warmer climate, but not the severe heat of Tashkent. Recalled Danilov: "I needed a city in which there was a circus…a few large theaters, and a large library—and more than just one. The entire preference pointed to Alma-Ata."

On January 3, 1980, Danilov and his wife arrived in Alma-Ata, never having been in Kazakhstan before. When they left Magadan, it was 45 degrees below zero. When they arrived in Alma-Ata, they immediately noticed that outside there was still grass, "green and glistening." "Where have we arrived?" Danilov thought. This is my kind of place.

Danilov and his wife live in a modest apartment on a pension of 130 tenge a month, the equivalent of a little more than $10. His years of work in coal mines and countless hours tediously collecting and cataloging biographical data have exacted their toll. Even though his speech cracks with coughs, he speaks with emotion and deep pride about the work to which he has devoted his life.

The tiny bedroom that he has converted into his office is bursting with cards on his subjects. He concedes the limitations of his research: all of the information is in Russian, and he only opens a listing when he has the complete name and birth date on a subject. He then keeps cross-references on the subject from radio, television, and newspapers. Most of the work is keeping up cross-references on old subjects, rather than enlarging his list of subjects. But, when he meets potential subjects, he is not bashful about requesting that they fill out cards about themselves.

Danilov proudly showed me cards for many of his subjects, including Raisa Gorbachev and Nursultan Nazarbayev. Under his interests, Nazarbayev wrote that he enjoyed tennis and boasted a large private library, a point of special significance to Danilov, who attaches great meaning to the collection of books. Nazarbayev wrote and then curiously whited out that he played the dombra, a Kazakh folk instrument. Danilov thinks that the most interesting people he has watched in recent years include Olzhas Suleimenov, a poet turned politician; Dinmukhamed Kunaev, the former head of the Kazakhstan Communist Party; Sabit Mukhanov, a famous Kazakh writer who died in 1973; and Nazarbayev. When Danilov talks of Nazarbayev, he lowers his voice and utters what is on many ethnic Russians' minds: "I know that so long as Nazarbayev is working, nothing bad will happen. But if Nazarbayev weren't around, then only God knows what might happen."

In 1987, *Ogonek*, a Soviet newspaper, published an article about Danilov's work. An avalanche of mail ensued, sometimes just addressed to "Danilov, Alma-Ata." Over the next three years, Danilov received 26,000 pieces of mail. He personally responded to 14,000! A couple of years ago, there was a project in Russia to finance transferring to the computer the data Danilov has painstakingly maintained. Photocopying the materials produced 660 pounds of material. Twelve data entry technicians worked six months, completing just a third of the project, before the project ran out of money.

Danilov borrowed the name for his project from Gherman Titov, who, in August 1961, was the second person to orbit the Earth. Yuri Gagarin may have been the first person to orbit the Earth, but he was unable to look out at Earth. Titov viewed the Earth from the stratosphere and wrote a book entitled *My Blue Planet*. Danilov corresponded with Titov, who gave his permission to Danilov to use the name for Danilov's project. Ever since, Danilov's passion has had the name: "The People of the Blue Planet."

Before I left, Danilov asked me to fill out a card. I joined the other 250,000 personages in Danilov's files. I now have the burden to make something of my life. Danilov's health is failing. He has trouble breathing, and even walking is a chore. He gets by with his wife on a pension that is not enough even for the basic necessities. No one pays for his work, but he continues to labor 18 hours a day on his project. He has information on almost 250,000 people. His dream is to reach 300,000. What keeps him going? "I think that I am not ordinary. I have an insatiable appetite for information, and I love books."

◆   ◆   ◆

Better to Live in the Country

There is considerable discontent in the populace, especially when the disorder that pervades the city is obvious and visible. Planes are starved for fuel. The regular flights to Moscow, costing about 400 tenge or about $35, have been delayed because of the fuel shortage; the "commercial" flights on Transaero, the new Russian airline, costs three times as much, but it has a reputation for having fuel to fly.

In some parts of the city today, the hot water was turned off to save energy. It is snowing heavily, but the street cars are not even running. There are throngs waiting in the cold on every street corner. I was lucky to catch a taxi. The driver commiserated: "I told my wife long ago, we should live in a village, where you don't have to rely on anyone." The lady in the back seat added: "I heard that the communist leaders came out and said that there might have to be a civil war." She probably was referring to the Moscow media. To the older generation, despite independence, the former republics of the Soviet Union are still one big country.

A Little Bit of the Country in Almaty

I was at the corner of Mukanov and Toli Bi Streets at about 8:00 on a Sunday morning. The temperature was in the teens. There is a water pump on that particular corner. There were two women and a young man, each with a bucket. They each laid out a towel on the ground, filled their buckets with cold water, and stripped down to their bathing suits. The sun was barely peaking over the mountains to the South. They extended their arms towards the sun and poured the cold water over their bodies. After drying, they dressed and went about their business.

They perform this ritual twice a day. They are adherents of the Ivanov System, which purports to be an "integrated system of exercises for the health of one's body and soul." Scenes such as what I saw on that Sunday morning play out throughout the city. One particularly popular place is on the road to Medeo on the Malaia Almatinka, where the adherents take a quick dip in the freezing mountain stream.

Ivanov innovated this system of exercises for health decades ago. The system assumes that all that is needed to keep the body healthy is in the human organism. The system not only includes the ritual of pouring cold water over oneself twice a day, but also a weekly fast for at least 24 hours and no more than 72 hours. The system also requires abstinence from smoking and drinking. Even though Nazarbayev's wife is reportedly one of its adherents in Almaty, the system does not enjoy widespread popularity. It is not a system for the faint of heart.

Contact Lens Solution and a Safe

There are some minor conveniences of living in a city. I just returned from a triumphal visit to town, having found saline solution for my contact lenses. I ran out of saline solution a couple of weeks ago, but thought I might be able to obtain a local source when I saw an ad on television for contact lenses. I called the number and was told that the store has a "wide" selection of solutions.

Having been in Almaty already for five months, I should have known that a "wide" selection was not the same as the Payless Drug Store in California. The "store" was behind an apartment building in a small building. On the second floor, there was a small room and there were a few samples of contact lens solution.

The proprietor gave a great marketing pitch for each solution, about how they performed all kinds of miracles on your eyes. She went on for several minutes about each one. There were five different kinds of solution on display. They were all run-of-the-mill saline solutions for soft contact lenses. Only two kinds were in stock. The other three were for display only.

I asked the price. The cost in the U.S. would have been about $2–$4. When she quoted the price, I thought she meant 28 tenge. But she meant $28. That's a lot of money, I thought. Nothing like monopoly pricing. Actually, I got a bit of a break. They gave me a favorable exchange rate: 10 tenge to the dollar. The cost was 280 tenge or, at the free market exchange rate, $20. You cannot knock success. The success was finding the lens solution, not paying five times the price for the same item as in the U.S.

We then went into an office to conclude the transaction. She kept the saline solution…in a safe. I gave her the money in exchange for the precious solution.

The Kiosk System

Very little of the vigorous energy in this budding market is directed to producing anything. One of my students cited an article in which only 7 percent of the economic activity in the country is directed to manufacturing. I do not know the accuracy of his statistics, but virtually all of the goods in the kiosks and stores are foreign made.

The inefficiencies in this emerging market would make any economist cringe. This would not be news for anyone who has taken a trip to Moscow. There is a certain hierarchy of stores. At the bottom of the distribution system are the old women standing on street corners hawking a few goods. They stand there all day with a few goods stretched out in front of them. They all sell essentially the same goods: cigarettes, matches, and vodka.

Woman trying to sell a few things in a make-shift kiosk.

Then there are the kiosks. The kiosk system: prospective purchasers scan the goods through the glass window. All kiosks have ample supplies of vodka and cigarettes, but there the similarity ends. Some have juices, soda, and crackers. Others have wine (no California wines) and chocolates. A few even have some food such as canned peas or spaghetti. Products come and go. One day, you can find all the sodas you want, and then they will disappear for weeks or even months. The goods are displayed with their prices in the window. After you have identified the goods you want, you need to memorize what you want, stand in line, and through a small window, like a teller at the bank, you need to recite the goods you want.

There are usually several people in the kiosk—not to help process your order, but to keep the proprietor company or, in some cases, as protection. Many kiosk owners spend the night in their kiosks, worried (and there is substantial concern) that someone could rip them off in the night or, for those who don't pay the protection money, burn down the kiosk. For those without large inventories, it is not unusual for the kiosk owner to remove everything from the kiosk late at night and return the following day.

Then there are the "trading houses," little larger than kiosk, housed in one room of an apartment house on the ground floor. These are generally small, with a hodgepodge of goods. There usually is one style of jacket in one size. If it's not your size, you can't really say, "Do you have a larger size?" There is no rhyme or reason for the appearance of certain goods. They just come and go. They have clothes and makeup, sometimes even a pair of skis. These are friendlier places. If you find something you want, you had better buy it right away. There is no telling when or whether you will find it somewhere else.

At the top of the hierarchy are larger trading houses with Western goods. There are a few around town. Even the sole department store in town is starting to get more Western goods. I bought my hat there, probably at about 5–10 percent more than the *barakholka*, the swap meet, but at least I had a chance to try several on and make a decision without five people telling me how this was the best hat in the world for me, that it fit me perfectly, when in fact it was falling down over my eyes.

Shopping Is an Art for Those with Good Memories

The government system functions alongside the private system. Food stores are dreary. Each store has its own specialty. Some sell bread, some sell dairy products, and some sell meat. And some larger government stores have separate counters for these primary food groups.

But government stores are only for those who have good memorization skills. The shopper first must decide what he or she wants to buy, then go to the cashier, and recite the products. If it is not one of the more common products, it is better also to memorize the prices. You have to maintain your composure even if you falter. There may be some less than patient shoppers also waiting in line, and their short-term memory skills may be acting at capacity. You obtain the receipt, present the receipt back at another counter, collect the goods, and get to go home, but only if you haven't forgotten anything.

◆   ◆   ◆

A Little Piece of Americana Goes Awry

The weather has taken a slide—way down the thermometer. It will probably get down to below zero, which is very cold for Almaty. I was asked to interview candidates for Muskie Fellowships this past week. The Muskie Fellowship assists students in the former Soviet Union to come to the U.S. for further studies in law, business, and public administration.

The American woman who helps to administer the program here in Almaty is meticulously organized. Another lawyer who is the Soros Foundation's representative in Almaty was also tapped to interview candidates. We just needed to wait for the three representatives from the program who had come from the U.S. and were in Moscow for interviews.

The program schedule was worked out well in advance. There were two minor problems: the weather and fuel. The U.S. representatives were due here on Monday on the more reliable non-Aeroflot flight, Transaero, which flies twice a week. We had a huge snowfall on Monday, preventing the plane from landing. The plane had to land in Karaganda, an hour north of here by plane. O.K., so the interviews would be postponed a few hours. For those leaving Almaty on the return leg to Moscow, they would have to come back to the airport late Monday afternoon instead of Monday morning.

It all sounded very plausible, except it was all a lie. The plane had never taken off from Moscow, and the Transaero representative was perpetuating this lie. And the Muskie Fellowship representative in Almaty unwittingly passed on this lie to the 60 applicants, who were waiting for their 15-minute interview to show that they were worthy of U.S. financial support to study in the U.S. Do you get the idea?

This was the chance to show how well the Americans do it, but, because of the lie, we did to these unwitting candidates what the Soviets did for seven decades. Every day the Transaero flight was supposed to arrive, and every day for three days it did not arrive. On Thursday, the plane finally came to Almaty, minus one of the Muskie Fellow representatives who could no longer come to Almaty. The applicants waited an extra three days. Some had come from all over the country (remember this country is as large as the entire Western U.S.). One of the people I interviewed was from Karaganda. He had to return to work to Karaganda while he waited. Karaganda is about 400 miles north of here. The airports are out of fuel. He came for his interview in a military helicopter, the only way he could have made it to his interview.

The interview schedule was entirely out of sync. Applicants called every day, sometimes several times, to find out the schedule. The delays, of course, had disrupted their lives for the entire week. They waited for their interviews in the corridor, some for several hours, as we tried to recreate the interview schedule. The auditorium where we conducted the interviews was cold, the temperature probably not rising above the fifties. We had done to these applicants what had been done to them all their lives. We had failed to create our little island of sanity in this sea of chaos. Nevertheless, we made sure we completed all of the interviews. It was 8:00 PM when we finished the last interview.

From Kiev to Almaty

The "official" word is that the airport will be closed another *eleven days,* because there is no fuel for the planes. The U.S. embassies in various republics called for reinforcements in preparation for the impending visit of President Clinton to Russia, Belarus, and Ukraine. Some of the embassy staff went off to Belarus. Another woman went off to the embassy in Kiev. There are no direct flights between Kiev and Almaty.

Her flight schedule required her to fly to Moscow. Moscow flights have been delayed first for the weather and then because of a lack of jet fuel.

The U.S. Embassy in Almaty wanted its employee back after the president's visit. She was, however, stranded in Kiev. The only way to retrieve her was to authorize her to fly to Frankfurt and take the Lufthansa flight to Almaty. If you are not familiar with the locations of these cities, take a look at a map. She did not take the most direct route home!

Making Ticket Reservations... Will I Be Able to Leave?

I am busy trying to make reservations to the U.S. It is almost a full-time job. There is no Delta office here. The closest office is in Moscow. The only problem is getting through by telephone. I have tried repeatedly for a few days. Even when I get a line and the call goes through, no one answers the phone.

Kazakhstan has its own airline, an offshoot of Aeroflot, the old Soviet airline. Kazakhstan Airlines (or Kazakhstan Aue Zholy, in Kazakh) has flights to Germany, but I have not been able to get through to the information number. I called the old Aeroflot booking number. The voice barked back: "Talk." "I would like to find out about flights to Germany," I inquired. Another bark came out of the receiver: "No, we only do flights within the [Soviet] Union." She was kind enough to give me another number, but no one has answered that telephone.

◆   ◆   ◆

Soros Foundation—Meet the Soros Club

I attended a reception at the U.S. Embassy in honor of the Central Election Commission of Kazakhstan and a visiting delegation of congressional staffers who were in Almaty to give a brief seminar for those involved in the upcoming elections. After the reception, I was invited to the Soros Club.

U.S. Embassy in Almaty.

The Soros Club is a grassroots organization that was established in Almaty in about 1991. It has no connection whatever to the Soros Foundation. Since George Soros established the Foundation, through which George Soros has donated tens of millions of dollars for the cause of democracy in formerly socialist countries, many people have tried to exploit the Soros name for their own ends with nothing to do with the philanthropic purposes of the Soros Foundation.

The Soros Foundation's representatives came to Almaty and saw an advertisement about the Soros Foundation building a university in Almaty. There was one minor problem: the Soros Foundation had no connection with the advertisement or this phantom university. After a brief investigation, the Foundation's representatives learned that some locals were simply trying to raise some money using the Soros name.

During this same visit to Almaty, the Soros Foundation representatives learned of the Soros Club, and understandably they viewed the Soros Club with some skepticism. But they learned that the Soros Club is not out for money; its mission is to bring people together for an exchange of views on culture and politics.

The Soros Club is the creation of Mikhail Pavlovich Shmulev, who, with his long, thick gray hair parted down the middle and bushy eyebrows, looks the part of an old hippie. His full face looks sun worn, and, when he smiles, his eyes almost close. Shmulev lives by himself in an ornate two-story home on the outskirts of town. (A short aside: apartments are more expensive than most stand-alone houses/hovels, primarily because the bathrooms for these small houses are not inside the houses.) Shmulev's house is adorned with paintings, books, and medals on every wall. There are even aphorisms decorating various walls and ceilings. The ceiling in the living room has portraits of women in literature and the arts. One wall is graced with portraits of Nobel Prize winners and, of course, a portrait of George Soros.

Shmulev does not know his birth date, other than that he was born three years before Lenin died. He lived his early years with his stepmother on a collective farm in western Siberia. When he was 14, Shmulev fled the "difficult life" of the collective farm, hopping the rails to Kazakhstan. He arrived in Alma-Ata in 1936. The government had just commenced its program of industrialization in the region, and the Alma-Ata that Shmulev saw was still a small town of one-story houses. Shmulev commented with some irony: "The communists say they built up this area; yes, but they did it with slave labor." Shmulev lived the life of a hobo, sleeping on park benches and working odd jobs before World War II.

In 1939, Shmulev was drafted into the Soviet army. It is no secret anymore that Soviet soldiers donned uniforms of other military forces to mask their activities. Shmulev wore the uniform of the Finnish People's Army and later became part of the occupying force of Latvia. Shmulev was lightly wounded in 1941. After recovering, he spent a few years in the Urals, teaching at a military school.

Shmulev returned to the front in 1944 and served in Rumania and Hungary. He was seriously wounded in Hungary. His comrades left him for dead. The Germans took him prisoner and confined him to a hospital in Hungary. He was in the hospital three and a half months, before he was sent to a prisoner-of-war camp. He escaped once but was recaptured. After his second effort to escape was successful, Shmulev returned to the Soviet Union, and he was immediately enlisted to go to China to train the Chinese on "how to organize an army."

In 1947, Shmulev returned to Alma-Ata, but within months he was arrested. His trial lasted five minutes. Shmulev was sentenced to eight years in a Stalinist labor camp. His crime was to be caught by the Germans. Remembered Shmulev: "An officer does not have the right to be a prisoner. He has no right to surrender." He added, as if he needed to explain his actions, "I didn't surrender. I was wounded on the battlefield."

Shmulev was not healthy enough to be sent to the camps in the Magadan region of the Soviet Far East. He went to one of the camps known as the Karaganda Camps, which Shmulev described as a "colossal empire" including camps throughout Kazakhstan and Uzbekistan. Shmulev's camp was near Karaganda. Eloquent in his other descriptions, Shmulev had few words to convey the conditions in the camp: "It was terrible, very bad...I don't even know how to describe terrible."

The Stalinist camps were emptied following Stalin's death in 1953. Shmulev had served six and a half years of his sentence. He was one of the lucky prisoners. He survived. When asked about his reaction to Stalin's death, his expressive face broke out in an ironic grin. "The tyrant is dead, the despot. Great." He applauded and looked up as if to thank God for his deliverance. "The communists cried. We were happy. At last—great, freedom."

Shmulev eventually returned to Alma-Ata in 1960, where he has lived for 34 years. He worked for the government, all the while building his house and building his various collections. In the past 15 years, Shmulev has hosted meetings at his house for the intelligentsia, artists, poets, authors, and others. Shmulev is certain that his telephone was tapped. "If there was not the August putsch [in Moscow in 1991], I can guarantee you that they would have arrested me."

In 1992, Shmulev transformed these meetings into the Soros Club. There are no official members of the Soros Club. The Club simply provides an outlet for the intelligentsia to share their views in the intimate confines of Shmulev's house. Why did Shmulev name his meetings in honor of George Soros? Shmulev explained:

"I was in Budapest in the hospital....I loved Hungary. When I went on a pension, I read a book by Soros. That is a great man, I thought....I started comparing my life with Soros. In 1945, I was in Budapest. Soros was there too. In 1947, I returned from China. They arrested me. In 1947, the communists went to Hungary. Soros emigrated to the West. He studied at universities in Europe and America. I studied at the camps. It is a very interesting analogy. Soros finished the university and started as a businessman, as a financier. I finished the camp university. I started a small collection of stamps, coins. Soros started collecting dollars...[Soros said that] when he started making more than he spent, he started helping formerly communist countries. I went on a pension. And then what? I have to open my collection to people."

Shmulev described his close kinship with Soros as if he were talking about a close friend. He spoke with little bitterness of the hardships he has endured. The Soros Club is an outlet for him to share his verve for life. What is his angle? Does he want a million from Soros? Shmulev would likely be content with an autograph from George Soros.

◆   ◆   ◆

The Three Questions of the Election

The election campaign is starting in earnest. The major Russian language weekly magazine has offered its readers the three defining questions of this campaign. It wants a simple yes or no answer to these questions:

1. Under the Constitution of the Republic Kazakhstan, land is the exclusive province of state ownership. Do you agree that in Kazakhstan there must be private ownership of land?

2. In accordance with the Constitution of the Republic Kazakhstan, the state language is Kazakh. Russian is the language of discourse between nationalities. Does it follow that Russian—the language of the majority of the population of Kazakhstan—should have the status of a state language equal with Kazakh?

3. Do you think that the power of president should be balanced by the power of parliament and an independent judicial system?

You probably can guess the answer that the editors of the newspaper want to elicit.

How Not to Get Elected

The garbage is piling up again. The city is not even providing this basic service. Not since the cholera outbreak has the garbage piled up so high. If the government is trying to convince people to vote for the status quo, it should figure out a way to pick up the garbage.

A few years ago, I was visiting a law school classmate in Chicago. He had forsaken the law in favor of politics and was working for Mayor Daley. We were discussing some of the global issues of the day when he turned to me and told me that nuclear disarmament and world hunger were important issues, but the major issue in Chicago was abandoned cars. The average voter in Chicago chooses candidates not on global issues, but rather on the ability of the city government to get rid of abandoned cars quickly. The city administration of Almaty could take a lesson in election politics from some of our elected city officials in the U.S.

No Parliament—but New Laws

There is no parliament and, theoretically, no legislative branch of government. The president rules by decree, mostly on matters of national importance, before the new parliament is seated, or so I thought. The president raised the upper limit on taxes from 40 percent to 60 percent. I have not seen the decree, but it exceeds the authority Nazarbayev was expected to exercise before the new parliament was elected.

Less surprising was the removal of Judge Aidmikhalibetov from the Supreme Court, despite the constitutional provision that judges are independent and "subordinate only to the Constitution and laws of the Republic of Kazakhstan." He was the judge at the Lawyers' Conference who spoke against Shaikenov's legal reform package. Aidmikhalibetov landed an ambassadorship as his compensation. The more things change, the more they seem the same.

◆   ◆   ◆

Constitution Day—but Who's Celebrating?

The news on the first ever Constitution Day, a national holiday observed on January 28, was that no one had much of a clue what was being celebrated, other than a day off work. Workers got the day off work to stroll the streets and enjoy munificent meals with their families, but there was little in the way of observing the meaning of the day. The Constitution of Kazakhstan is long on words and short on specific guarantees. It offers a shopping cart full of broad guarantees from leisure, housing, health protection, social security, and education to a natural environment "favorable to life and health." Nazarbayev indicated that the document was intended as a transitional document, and substantial amendments are expected before the end of 1994.

The Constitution crowned the Kazakh language as the official state language, resisting the example of Switzerland, Canada, or even Israel, where there is more than one official language. Russian, the language of the majority of Kazakhstanis, was relegated to the language of discourse between nationalities. Most parliamentarians, even the majority of Kazakhs, required headphones to listen to the Russian interpretation of proceedings in the last parliament.

Only those having a command of the "state language" may be elected as president, vice president, or chairman of the Supreme Soviet. I once asked a friend her attitude if a non-Kazakh, who knew the state language, were elected president. She is well educated and has close friends who are not Kazakhs. Nevertheless, she replied tersely: "Very negatively." Her response probes the degree of tolerance of many Kazakhs towards non-Kazakhs.

Russians, and especially young Russians, have reacted strongly to this sentiment, and many are intent on leaving. As they contemplate their futures, they have told me on several occasions, "Kazakhstan is for Kazakhs," or "Russians are of a second sort here." With the somber memory of other multiethnic communities, such as Sarajevo or Baku, the ethnic climate in Kazakhstan seems the perfect recipe for disaster. In response to this threat, the president and many other Kazakhs speak passionately about the moral imperative to treat the Russians as equal partners in building this new country. The possibility of Kazakhstan to make a smooth transition to a democracy rests on Nazarbayev's ability to prevail on his Kazakh countrymen to embrace all ethnic communities as equals.

6

Venturing out of Almaty

February 1994

A Mile High out of Almaty

I have been agitating to see the other cities of Kazakhstan. My enthusiasm, however, has been tempered by my understanding that traveling is not a sport for the short-winded. Every time I have flown within the former Soviet Union, it has been a unique experience. Last time I was leaving Almaty in 1991, I was on my way to Moscow…

There I was, waiting patiently for a toilet on board the Soviet-made aircraft. Anyone who has been on an Aeroflot trip knows how small and disgusting the lavatories are. There were two stocky guys talking with one another. One was a redhead and had a well-groomed mustache. When one of the toilets became free, I started making a move towards the toilet, thinking that these two guys were just talking. But one of the men darted in front of me; and his friend was quick to follow. There these two guys were in the bathroom. They could not even close the door all the way, although nothing was visible. I heard some banging noises emanating from inside the lavatory. I will leave it to the imagination of the reader what endeavors in which they may have been engaged in the bathroom. I will not jump to any conclusions. They never succeeded in locking the door. Probably it was too much of a squeeze inside; but they emerged about ten minutes later, both smiling.

The mile-high club is only one of many stories on Aeroflot. I recognized that traveling inside of Kazakhstan meant that I would have to fly on the successor to Aeroflot in Kazakhstan, Kazakhstan Airlines. I did not have any illusions that the traveling would be easy, and I was right.

I got my wish to travel outside of Almaty and venture out to some of the other cities in Kazakhstan. I selected Karaganda, the home of Karaganda State University and the center of the coal industry in Kazakhstan.

An Auspicious Start

The weather had been warming up in Almaty until the day of my trip to Karaganda. The snow started falling in the morning with virtually no break. In the afternoon, it began to fall very heavily. I was dubious about whether I would be able to leave Almaty. I called the airport for some guidance. "Oh, yes, come on down, we are running on schedule," said the information operator at the airport. I had no choice. My driver came and we plodded through the icy roads to the airport. My flight was supposed to leave at 8:30 PM. I arrived at about 7:30. No sooner had I entered the terminal, when I heard an announcement: the flight to Karaganda had been delayed until midnight.

Meanwhile, one of the vice rectors of the university, Kairzhan Beki-shev Bekimevich, had been drafted to greet the American guest. He and a driver drove through a wind storm in temperatures dropping down to 30 degrees below zero—without the wind chill. They waited expectantly for their guest from America. They dared not leave the car for fear that they would not be able to get it started if they turned it off. After waiting a couple of hours, they heard the news that I had been delayed and would arrive after 1:00 AM. They returned to the city to wait for a while and then to come back to the airport later.

I must confess that I expected the delay. I thought about going home, but I recognized that there were probably some poor souls at the airport waiting to greet me. I had no choice but to stick it out. The "locals" who had paid 100 tenge, about $8, for their tickets waited in the main terminal, stretched out on battered chairs or lying on the ground. Foreigners who paid $81 could wait in the "Intourist" lounge with its bar in an adjacent building.

The only foreigners in the bar besides me were two young men from Lithuania who had taken up residence in Kazakhstan to wheel and deal on the metals markets. At least with a few warm bodies in the bar, it was somewhat warm. I had struck up a conversation with the two Lithuanians, only one of whom was going to Karaganda. The other was seeing him off. They graphically described their exploits both on and off the battlefield of "commerce." They were both in their early twenties, although their faces showed more years. One of them has been in Kazakhstan for three years and eagerly told of the deals he had concluded.

I asked him about the common perception that one can only get things done through local contacts. He laughed. The only local contact one needs is money, he told me. With enterprise directors getting the equivalent of a few hundred dollars a month, they are eager to accept illicit contributions. According to this entrepreneur, the first deal is the most difficult, but subsequent deals flow easily. The size of the bribes: in the tens of thousands of dollars. I asked about the recent introduction of the strict tariffs. He told me that he gets them reduced to zero. One can't get anything done in this country by complying with the law. He was a very soft-spoken man, not a wild cowboy on the frontier. He was just relating the facts.

At a little past 11:00 PM, we were informed that the flight had been delayed until 2:40 AM. When the bar closed at midnight, we were all evicted to the unheated lounge area, which was dark and very cold. My Lithuanians friends decided to go home and return later. I stayed and lay down on a couch. I stretched my Russian hat over my ears to keep my head warm and buttoned my jacket to the top button. I faded in and out of sleep, as people started to filter in to meet the Lufthansa flight from Frankfurt, which was scheduled to arrive in the early morning hours.

Back in Karaganda, the vice rector of the university and his driver had returned to the airport to meet the flight that was not destined to arrive any time soon. They remained in the car, waiting expectantly for their guest from America for another few hours. Then they got the news that the flight would not arrive until after 7:00 AM. They were running low on gas, as the car had been running all the time. They went home.

We finally got to the plane at about 2:30 AM. It was completely enveloped with snow and ice, and the runway was barely visible. Was any of this really worth it, I thought? The deicing truck came, a reminder of civilization. The flight was packed, and there were not enough seats for all the passengers. As the flight crew sorted out these problems, we sat on the tarmac for another hour, gathering ice and making the deicing exercise useless. I was so tired anyway that I do not even remember the take-off.

We arrived in Karaganda. It was after 5:00 AM. I had a hint of what was to come when I boarded the bus to go to the terminal. There was one-half foot of snow on the *floor of the bus*. The terminal looked ultra-modern, but, when we got in it, I wasn't sure whether we were inside or outside. Some of the passengers made a break for the street and another building across the street. I followed. There were a couple of cars, but, after I inquired of the drivers, I learned that none was from the university. I was not surprised. The wind howled. The skin on my face felt like it would peel off. It was 30 below and I had arrived in Karaganda in the darkness and in the middle of a blizzard sweeping across the steppe.

How Do You Spell Cold?...K-a-r-a-g-a-n-d-a

Karaganda is a city surrounded by the remnants of Stalin's camps. Virtually the only industry is coal. Karaganda has one of the most inhospitable climates I have ever experienced. The remnants of Stalinist camps surround the city, and a stay in Karaganda reinforces the impression that Stalin was adept at picking punishing places for his camps.

If an American in Karaganda can be lucky, I was lucky. There were two cars waiting for people and over a hundred passengers. As I inquired of one of the drivers whether he was headed towards town, he agreed to take me to my hotel. My new Lithuanian friend joined us. The other passengers would have to fend for themselves.

The driver, Illaraion, was picking up his daughter. He was one of two drivers to endure the elements and wait until our delayed plane finally landed. There was one minor problem: I did not have the name of the hotel. We drove in Illaraion's Japanese-made Sambar towards the city, as the wind blew the snow across the road. Every once in a while, the car would hit a couple of feet of snow in the road. Illaraion did not even slow down.

I had heard that there were only two decent hotels in town: the Chaika and the Kosmonatov. The others barely have heat and are teaming with prostitutes. It was too cold for cockroaches! Yes, this was my lucky morning. We decided to try the Kosmonatov. Without a reservation from a local organization, there is no way to obtain a room. There was a letter from the university, but it did not appear to have my name. At 6:00 in the morning, who cares? I had planned on staying two nights, but I had already spent one of the nights at the airport terminal. The woman was friendly and charged me for just one night…at the rate reserved for Kazakhstanis of 48 tenge, or about $4. The rate for foreigners was $50, but I must have qualified as an honorary Kazakhstani on this day.

Illaraion asked whether the rooms were well heated. The woman replied that they had warm blankets. We all knew what she meant. There were no icicles in the room, but it was probably a good temperature for milk and eggs. I climbed into bed with several layers of clothing and pulled the much advertised warm blanket over my head. I had arrived.

I slept for a few hours. The security guard downstairs told me, "before, under the Soviets, everything was OK." It was only the new order that had brought chaos. I did not have the telephone number for my contact at the university. Unlike Almaty, I could not call from Karaganda directly to Almaty. I needed to order a line, which took more than an hour. After failing to make contact with the university, I readily agreed to Illaraion's offer to show me the sights of Karaganda.

The Sights of Karaganda

The scenery was bleak at best. The skies were gray and the buildings drab. The only interesting looking building was a new mosque, which was almost complete. The endless rolling hills around Karaganda used to be flat steppe. Illaraion told me that there were villages all around Karaganda, but the mining caused the earth to collapse. The ground swallowed the villages, leaving rolling hills. We visited the Gorbachev Coal Enterprise (not *that* Gorbachev) and met with the head of the labor collective. The coal enterprise still boasted a sign over its entrance: "Glory to Coal Labor." He indicated that the labor unions had to nominate their own candidates because the Socialist Party had not elicited the support of the labor unions. The head of the labor collective indicated that he would gladly support the Socialist Party candidates, but it was up to the Socialist Party to come to him, not the other way around. He was dubious about the prospects of any of the labor collective's candidates winning and seemed to imply that he expected some irregularities in the voting.

Gorbachev Coal Enterprise in Karaganda.

I also had a chance to meet with some of the miners who had just decided to delay a strike, after reaching a compromise with Prime Minister Sergei Tereshenko. They were not enthusiastic about the agreement, but they seemed pleased that they would finally receive their wages, which had been delayed for as long as a couple of months. I observed the miners coming up from their shifts. They work in six-hour shifts, four shifts a day, three working and one for repair work. Shifts are comprised of about 700 workers. They gather in a building to discuss their work assignments and then take elevators into the bowels of the earth. Instead of trolleys, as in the West, they walk to their assignments, sometimes taking as long as 40 minutes.

When I saw these miners at the end of their shift, they were completely blackened. It was hard to distinguish any human features other than the whites of their eyes. The mines are great equalizers. The only thing distinguishing the head of the work group is the white helmet. Other than that meager class distinction, all miners are equal. They rushed out from the elevator through the cold to showers. Some work in the "warm" areas where it is 50–55 degrees, others in colder conditions.

End of the shift at the coal mines.

Why do they subject themselves to this work? The pay is about 1500 tenge, roughly $110 a month, as much as four times the average monthly wage. Even though their lives are foreshortened by their work, they eagerly work for the extra pay and then live on their pensions. Pensions start at age 50, which is not surprising, when one considers that the average life expectancy for a miner is about 52. According to a Western coal expert in Karaganda, John Marunich, the death rate in Karaganda mines is as much as 20 times as high as that in the U.S., one fatality per million tons mined.

There are 24 mines and three open pits in and around Karaganda. The ash content is about 38 percent, in sharp contrast to the world standard of about 10 percent. Fly ash from stacks causes huge health and environmental problems, as do refuse piles. The good news is that the sulfur content is low, less than 1 percent.

The concentration of methane in the mines is extraordinarily high. The methane gas leaks up from the mines. A few years ago, 120 were killed in an explosion. My driver said that, if you are a smoker, you should be very careful when lighting your cigarette in any of the villages around Karaganda. It may be your last smoke.

Head of the District Election Commission

I wanted to meet with election officials in Karaganda. Most refused to meet with me. Foreigners are still viewed with suspicion in Karaganda. But one election official agreed to meet with me. He was the head of one of the district election commissions. He was quick to offer that he was an associate professor who had no background in elections. He was not paid for his work, and his commission was severely understaffed.

His district had declined to register two candidates because of signature irregularities on the petitions. A candidate had to collect 3,000 signatures out of about 70,000 eligible voters in a district to earn a spot on the ballot. Many people were scared even to answer the door. I know I would not open a door for a stranger. In winter, there are few public places that people gather. Consequently, obtaining 3,000 signatures turned out to be a challenge for prospective candidates.

According to this election official, some candidates apparently tried to overcome this obstacle by falsifying signatures or having one member of the family signing for other members of the family. Some of those who signed the petition did not fill in their full name, disqualifying their signature.

The commission only had a week to verify the petitions of eight separate candidates, more than 24,000 signatures. There are only 11 commission members, and they can only verify signatures during evening hours when people are at home. He candidly told me that the commission verified only a few signatures. If the commission found that a large portion of those signatures were falsified (he did not define "large portion"), the commission refused to register the candidacy of those individuals. He indicated that those who were not registered were of some stature, and he expected some controversy to ensue.

The next stage of the election will be the campaign. Each of the candidates is limited to 6110 tenge, not even $500, for campaign spending. The individual with whom I met expected many questions about how to apply the law, and he thought that this aspect of the elections would be particularly hard to police. He optimistically predicted that the actual voting would proceed smoothly because of both the presence of international observers and the right of the candidates to have their own observers present during the counting of the ballots.

He candidly shared with me his thoughts on the political situation in the country: "We are not all that stable." According to this election official, the ethnic question stands as the most pressing problem of the time. The issues of dual citizenship and the standing of Russian as an official language loom as the most important issues of the campaign. He is particularly disturbed by the instability in and around Karaganda. Interestingly, of those registered in his district, six were Kazakhs, one Russian, and one Armenian. Even though he is Kazakh, he will vote for the Russian candidate and hopes that others will vote their conscience and not their ethnicity.

The election will be a free-for-all with unpredictable results. The system is a plurality system, in which the candidate with the most votes earns a seat in parliament. Many of the winning candidates, indeed probably most of the candidates, will garner a paltry plurality of the vote. There are some districts in which there are as many as six Kazakhs running against one Russian. The results in those districts are especially difficult to predict.

The government list was published. The list was comprised of 64 candidates: 24 non-Kazakhs and 40 Kazakhs. Two candidates will be elected from each district. Based on the ethnic mix in the various regions, there could be roughly 22 Kazakhs and 20 Russians elected from the presidential list.

The University

Virtually everyone I met at Karaganda State University was Kazakh, although I was told that the student population is about half Kazakh and half Russian. (Like most cities, especially in the North, the city is predominantly Russian.) In accord with Soviet practice, my schedule was organized only after I arrived.

I gave one lecture at the University, mostly to teachers. A few students attended. I talked generally about parallels between the U.S. and Kazakhstan and the development of the U.S. legal system. The questions were good and pointed. A constitutional law professor, Kabdulsamikh Aitkhozhin, asked particularly pointed questions about how to construct the legal infrastructure in a country with traditions so foreign to those of Western Europe and the U.S. He opined that Kazakhstan should look to the Asian models for guidance in developing its system. Aitkhozhin is a harsh looking man, as if he had come straight from the steppe into the classroom. Although not similar in appearance to constitutional law professors in the U.S., Aitkhozhin impressed me as being as intelligent as any of his counterparts in the West.

At Karaganda University.

Aitkhozhin seemed very interested in talking about some of the themes of the lecture, and he frequently appeared at my side until I caught the plane back to Almaty. Like many on my trip, he identified the "nationalities problem" as the most serious issue in Kazakhstan. We did not share the same point of view on all of the questions, but he impressed me, because he seemed to listen to a Western point of view. He had large gaps in knowledge about our system but nevertheless knew much about the U.S. Most literature is still from Soviet sources.

I finally met Kairzhan Bekimevich, the vice rector who made heroic efforts to meet me at the airport. He is in his early fifties, a nice man who took care of me, most likely because he had been drafted to take care of me. I gave him all of the materials on democracy and elections I had brought up with me, emphasizing that they were for the students. Of course, he asked me for his own copy of the materials. I agreed and Bekimevich immediately placed a set of materials into his safe. Bekimevich is also the head of the voting center at the University. Later in the day, when I was shown the voting center, some of the materials had already reached the glass case for display.

After my trip to Karaganda, I was pleased to return to civilization—Almaty.

◆　　◆　　◆

Nazarbayev Visiting Washington on Valentine's Day

Nazarbayev was going on a state visit to Washington, D.C. The ambassador gave a briefing to business people on the major topics that Nazarbayev would discuss with President Clinton. Ambassador Courtney is a major proponent of U.S.-Kazakhstan relations. At the briefing, Courtney argued that U.S.-Kazakhstan relations were the best in the former Soviet Union. The reason that the Administration remains committed to Kazakhstan is that the economic and political reforms are accelerating while Nazarbayev maintains a political consensus.

Courtney's comments add up to this: Nazarbayev would receive a substantial foreign aid package from Clinton.

◆   ◆   ◆

Privatization at a Snail's Pace

The privatization efforts have been proceeding slowly due to considerable resistance and bureaucratic bungling. Nevertheless, Nazarbayev has determined to accelerate the privatization effort, especially for 38 mammoth enterprises throughout the country. Western accounting and consulting firms are bidding for the opportunity to package these enterprises and lead them through the privatization process.

Medium-sized firms are also the subject of privatization, as they are being converted to joint stock companies before being sold off to investment funds, of which there will be about 100. Individuals then get to invest in these investment funds. The state will retain ownership of the enterprises through so-called holding companies of about 30 percent or more of these companies. Labor collectives get a miserly 10 percent. This type of privatization will likely not go very well.

Small shops and stores will also be privatized. Pilot auctions have been held in several parts of the country. But they have hit a roadblock. Someone has been trying to derail them. The bidders place on deposit 20 percent of the opening price. But the ultimate winning bid has been much higher, as much as ten times as high. The winning bidder then has 30 days to come up with the rest of the money; otherwise, he forfeits his deposit, and the property goes back to the auction block. Bidders have been bidding up the prices on these stores and then forfeiting their deposit so that nothing gets sold. These bidders apparently are intentionally trying to derail the auctions, although it is not clear why. And the beat goes on.

◆   ◆   ◆

Another Attack on an American

The foreign community in Almaty is small and as vulnerable as the locals to the increased criminal activity. There have been several attacks on foreigners since I arrived. On New Year's Eve, one of the construction workers on the new building for the U.S. Embassy was attacked in the stairway of his apartment. Even though he gave the robbers everything they wanted, they still pistol-whipped him. It is that kind of gratuitous violence that sends a shock wave through the foreign community.

We recently suffered another casualty. Eric Rudenshiold is the Almaty representative of the International Republic Institute, a project funded through the U.S. Agency for International Development. The Institute recently sponsored a series of seminars for political organizations participating in the upcoming elections. A few days ago, Rudenshiold was walking home from a hotel at about 10:00 at night. It was only a few blocks to his apartment. He was just down the street from the U.S. Embassy when he was accosted on the street. Rudenshiold had a flashlight and hit his attacker over the head, but then several others came up from behind Rudenshiold. One of these assailants had a gun—not just any gun, but a silencer. The assailants tried to escort Rudenshiold into an alley, but Rudenshiold refused, fearing that he would be killed. The attackers struck their American victim severely. Rudenshiold fell to the ground, playing dead. They kicked him several times before they left. They did not take any money.

Rudenshiold believes that this attack was politically motivated. Irrespective of the motive for the attack, the incident underscores the dangers to which we are exposed in this far away land. When one of our number is attacked, it exacts a heavy psychological toll from each of us and persuades many of us to stay home in the evenings.

Entertainment without an Audience

Theater and concerts in the evening attract paltry audiences. There are several deterrents: crime, poor transportation, lack of interest. I recently went to the symphony. The national symphony played an excellent program of Borodin and Shastokovich (who was not one of the more popular composers under the Soviet era). There were probably just as many people on stage, maybe even more with the choir, than there were in the audience. Even when Kazakhstan was part of the Soviet Union, few people attended the theater, regardless of whether it was the Russian or Kazakh theater. The price is not a major deterrent; tickets are the equivalent of about 30 cents.

It is almost painful that few people appreciate these wonderful performances. The theater cannot survive without some support from the community. As it is now, the symphony, opera, and ballet could disappear tomorrow, and I am afraid that hardly anyone would notice.

A Respite and Relief at a Concert

I went to a friend's birthday party, a major affair, possibly the most important annual celebration. People prepare for the party for weeks ahead of time. Next to me sat an attractive Kazakh man with a boyish face and graying hair. His name was Alibek Dnishev. I was told that he could sing, and, with little prompting, he sang for hours in tribute to the celebration. Much to my surprise, when I recounted the story to other friends, they were visibly impressed, even envious, that I had shared an evening with Alibek Dnishev. I learned that Dnishev is a household word, one of the luminaries of modern Kazakh culture.

I later went to a performance Dnishev gave at the Opera and Ballet Theater. I have regularly attended concerts in Almaty, and this was the first concert in which there was some energy, some magic in the crowd. It was the first time that I have seen the theater packed; usually, there are more people on stage than in the audience.

It seemed like every girl and woman and even some men had flowers for Dnishev. The audience exuded warmth, and Dnishev responded with a lively and emotional performance of Kazakh, Russian, and Italian opera. He introduced every piece himself with warmth and humor. The audience loved him. He did not turn away from what he had learned in this former Soviet republic. He sang with pride from Russian composers and even Soviet composers and was all but openly hostile to some contemporary composers.

The Dnishev concert, like many concerts, was recorded for television. The television folks wanted to get pictures of the audience. At each side of the stage, there were huge camera lights pointed directly, not at the stage, but at the audience. One hint for going to a concert in Almaty: sunglasses. I know now why Michael Jackson always wears sunglasses at his concerts.

The cultural life of this city is exploring new themes, but the Soviet influence still weighs heavily on the scene. The Dnishev concert was a good example. A private company sponsored the concert. In honor of the father of the company's president, the concert organizers gave out one of his novels for free. Yet, Dnishev's piano accompanist had to sit on two ugly red chairs stacked on top of one another. Even if there were a bench, it was obviously too low. This was not just a one-time problem. At several of the concerts I have attended, the chair of choice is the two-stacked red chair variant.

There was another curious aspect of the concert. The stage was beautifully decorated, draperies coming in from the sides, a huge and magnificent chandelier hanging down from the ceiling over the stage. But there was one blight on the stage. To the left of the chandelier, hanging out of place was a sign promoting the sponsor of the concert: Alemsystem. It was not one of these subtle, subliminal signs, but a huge sign (in Latin letters): ALEMSYSTEM. Just as the listeners were letting the concert take them to another world, the sign jarred them back into reality.

◆   ◆   ◆

Plane to Freedom

I took a brief trip to Europe for some rest and relaxation—to decompress. I was ready for a short break, especially after I received a call from the Management Academy's "first department" (the department for internal security) threatening to report me to the authorities for not having the required residence permit. I explained that the Management Academy had agreed to secure the residence permit months earlier, but, despite my requests and requests from the U.S. Embassy, the Management Academy had failed to obtain the residence permit on my behalf.

At the airport in Almaty, as I was waiting for the plane to Frankfurt, I called the Embassy to report the threat from the Management Academy. As I was talking on the phone, a man was impatiently waiting to use the phone. I was speaking on the phone in English, and he did not know I knew Russian. But he was very descriptive in his body language as to what he wanted me to do and as to the sanction for not following his direction to conclude my conversation immediately. I was ready to leave the country for a brief respite.

After we were on the plane, the man who had been waiting for the phone came to find me. He apologized for his conduct in the terminal. I told him that he should forget about it, but he informed me that, if I really forgave him, we had to drink some of his cognac. I obliged.

◆   ◆   ◆

And Back to Karaganda

I hesitate to write this entry as I am stuck on the runway in Karaganda, on my way back to Almaty from Frankfurt, Germany. The other passengers and I are just sitting on the plane, not knowing what fate awaits us. We are faced with three conditions, any of which would prevent us from taking off in the West. It is probably 10 below zero, not considering the wind chill. The plane was deiced, but that was a good hour ago. The wind is unrelenting. I don't know the speed, but some of the airport workers had trouble standing up outside. In any event, it was so windy that they have to walk backwards. And the only thing that seems to bother the pilot is the visibility, which is about zero.

Kazakhstan Airlines

The flight on Kazakhstan Airlines is one-third the price of Lufthansa. On the way to Frankfurt, the plane was only about one-third full. On the return, I was one of the last passengers to check in; I was number 29. A group of German tourists going to Almaty for a Speedway competition at Medeo brought the total passengers to about 35, out of a capacity of 350 on an Ilyushin Il-86 (in a single class layout).

There are three flights a week to Hannover, apparently filled to the gills, but only one way: Germans living in Kazakhstan are returning "home." They came to Russia in Catherine's time and, during World War II, were sent to Kazakhstan. The German population in 1989 reached almost one million, but now as many as 300,000 have already left Kazakhstan for Germany.

There is not much demand for the return flight from Hannover to Almaty. Similarly, there is a new flight to Vienna and Zurich, but, according to the flight attendant, she has flown on that route when there were only two (count them, two) passengers. There are other flights to Israel, Syria, China, Pakistan, and other places.

The food on Kazakhstan Airlines is passable. On this leg, the food comes from Frankfurt. The flight attendants are relatively friendly, but there is no nonsmoking section. Like on some U.S. airlines, the flight attendant woke me up to serve me a snack. I could have used the sleep. The leg room is immense, and I had the entire row to myself to sleep, except when the flight attendant woke me up.

We departed Frankfurt only about 30 minutes late, but we made up the time on the six and a half hour flight to Almaty. The weather in Almaty, however, would not cooperate. Snow in Almaty closed the airport; we were redirected to Karaganda, one of the few airports in the country that can accommodate this class of aircraft. We arrived at about 6:00 AM local time and were originally told that it would be 10:00 AM before we would be able to leave…then 2:00 PM…it is now almost 4:00 PM. We have been on the ground for about 10 hours (and on the plane for more than 16 hours), and the visibility is not getting any better.

"We Are Hostages"

It is now 7:00 PM. We are still on the runway in Karaganda. We haven't moved at all. The airport is open in Almaty, but we cannot take off here. The plane is quiet except for one of the Germans snoring very loudly. Every few minutes he talks in his sleep, in German of course, so I don't know what he is saying. I think we have watched the last movie on the screen, old "Twilight Zone" segments about Martians…appropriate, I thought.

The flight attendant informed me that the wind is blowing at 30 miles an hour outside. The wind has been battering the plane relentlessly, creating the sensation that we are flying. We are still on the runway. The good news is that the visibility has gotten no worse: it is still zero. The other good news: we took some passengers on who were supposed to fly from Karaganda to Almaty yesterday. At least if it gets really cold, they will be good to have around to keep warm, or if it gets really bad…(Did you ever see *Alive*, the movie about the passengers who resorted to cannibalism when they crashed in the Andes?)

A ground crew tried to place something on the engines to keep them from freezing. Because of the elements, they were not successful. As I understand it, even if it cleared up right now, we could not take off. You have the luxury of reading how this all comes out. As for me and the rest of the passengers, as of this writing, we have no clue how this will all end. As the flight attendant announced, "We are hostages."

Weather Report...9:00 PM

You could probably guess that we would still be here in Karaganda. The ground crew somehow found us and towed us back to the terminal. Now the engines are being warmed up and we are getting refueled. One of the engines was completely frozen, and a ground crew is working on it. The visibility has improved. We should land in Almaty, a one-hour flight, by—dare I predict—midnight.

You Were Wondering?

We took off at 11:27 PM. We were delayed on the ground in Karaganda for more than 17 hours (which was after more than 6 hours in flight). As we were readying for our takeoff, I saw three lonely figures on the tarmac. The snow from the steppe swept across the runway. The snow does not stick to the runway but creates the impression of dry ice on a stage, blowing at 30 miles an hour. The silhouettes of the three airport workers were evidence that there was some interest in having us leave Karaganda. The workers were probably happier than the passengers aboard the plane that we finally were able to take off. We were inside...and they were experiencing the full force of the steppe. If the roles were reversed, the past 17 hours could have been worse...When we arrived in Almaty, we had been on the plane for more than 24 hours.

◆   ◆   ◆

Motocross at Medeo

I had heard about Speedway when I was stuck on the runway in Karaganda. The German contingent stuck on the plane with me in Karaganda was traveling all the way from Frankfurt to Almaty to go to the "Speedway." What was this "Speedway" and what was it doing at Medeo, the world-class ice skating rink?

Medeo is a stadium built in 1972 at the foot of the Medeo Dam. The skating rink occupies a space in excess of 100,000 square feet, more than twice the size of a football field. The stadium holds 12,000 spectators. Weekends at Medeo are an experience. The youth of Almaty celebrate on the ice, skating, spinning and gyrating—and in the stands, rocking to the music. The place is alive with youthful spirit and energy.

Medeo on an average weekend.

But not this weekend. I thought that the Speedway might be a competition of snowmobiles, or cars on ice—wrong, wrong...Then I saw a poster with motorcycles. Admission was free. I wanted to witness first-hand why some spectators flew all the way from Germany to see the event.

Motocross at Medeo.

Flags of the participating states were flying in the cold breeze. The Czech Republic, Germany, Russia, Kazakhstan, and even the Netherlands were represented. To paint the start and finish on the ice, the maintenance man used a high tech precision instrument: a large paint brush. The anticipation mounted. The motorcycles broke the silence. Could these motorcycles really stay upright on the ice? They roared to the starting line and they were off, around the curves and down the straightaways. As the cyclists rounded the curves, their knees almost touched the ice, and, on the straightaways, the motorcyclists popped wheelies. I don't think I could have imagined motorcyclists on ice unless I saw it with my own eyes.

Strawberry Wine in the Mountains

Later in the day, a man I met invited me to his modest house near the stadium to share some wine. He built the small house with his own hands, and it looked like it. He was not an architect. The house sits precariously on the mountain. It looks like it would blow over in a mild breeze. There is no telling what a moderate earthquake would do to it. Fortunately, the sky was cloudless and the earth did not move while I enjoyed some of his homemade wine.

My host, Slava, makes ten different varieties of wine. We sampled the strawberry wine. It was not of California standard, but it was wholly drinkable. As we sat in his house, Slava shared his view of the election. He does not know who the candidates are, but, as for the government list, he thinks they are all old Party hacks, and he will vote against all of them. Slava represents the deep skepticism with which many view the elections.

Ribbons in the Trees…a Pagan Ritual?

On the road to Medeo, there are trees at the side of the road with ribbons tied to the branches. I have asked what the ribbons signify—and have received several interpretations. One interpretation is that those who have drunk or bathed in a water source for medicinal reasons return to the source and, as a tribute to the healing powers of the water source, attach a ribbon. Another interpretation is that those who simply want to mark that they have been to the spot attach a ribbon to a nearby tree. And the last interpretation is that Kazakh traditions are more pagan than Moslem and that Kazakhs attach a ribbon as a tribute to the gods.

◆   ◆   ◆

A Russian Wins a Gold Medal…for Kazakhstan

The 1994 Olympics in Norway concluded. The Kazakhstani flag was evident in the stands as Kazakhstanis ventured to Norway to support the first ever Olympic team from Kazakhstan. Vladimir Smirnov, an ethnic Russian, competed in the cross-country skiing events, winning the first ever gold medal for Kazakhstan.

The events were broadcast to Kazakhstan over Russian television. As Smirnov was racing, the Russian sports announcer could hardly contain his enthusiasm. Realizing that he might be too partisan for Smirnov, the announcer calmly told the viewing audience: "We of course are rooting for Smirnov because he is a talented sportsman"—right!

Ethnic consciousness permeates every aspect of life in the former Soviet Union—even in sports. Not long ago, I was watching Pete Sampras, the number one ranked tennis player in the world, on Russian television. Sampras, like me, hails from California. Although I am an avid tennis fan, I did not have the same insights as the Russian sports announcer. As Sampras approached the net to win a point, the television commentator remarked that he played the point as expected…because of his Greek background. Try that on me again.

And the National Basketball Association now does Moscow. I am not a big basketball fan, but I have watched some of the weekly highlights from N.B.A. action on Moscow television. Fortunately, the announcer has not commented on the ethnic background of the players. The program commentary is a direct translation of a U.S. television program without any "local" insights.

◆   ◆   ◆

The Elections

The elections are approaching. One aspect of the elections is certain: they are unpredictable. The local election commissions refused registration of several candidates because of an insufficient number of signatures or because of falsified signatures. Some candidates were probably not registered for political reasons, and some went to court and won their suits to get on the ballot. Some are still not on the ballot. The major problem areas are, not surprisingly, Almaty and Karaganda, where the local administrations run their cities in accordance with Soviet tradition. (The mayor of Almaty is entrenched in a battle with the local media—since one of the newspapers printed an open letter of a leading businessman accusing the mayor of Almaty of telling the head of internal affairs, that he, the businessman, was trying to assassinate the mayor.)

A candidate who was not registered in Karaganda is now on a hunger strike. There are 754 candidates, 64 on the so-called presidential list for 42 seats, and the remaining 690 for the remaining 135 seats. In some districts, there are as many as 13 running. About 75 percent of the candidates are Kazakh.

The candidates have 10 minutes on television, 10 minutes on radio, and small posters with their biographies and so-called platforms. The pictures on the posters are more akin to mug shots, like the WANTED posters you see in U.S. post offices. The pictures bear little resemblance to the candidates. The platforms are long on words and short on substance. Very few enlighten the voters on the candidate's views.

The ethnic composition of the new parliament will be a major indication of the stability of the country. There are already those who predict the worst. Last month, Olzhas Suleimenov, a leading Kazakhstani writer who is also running on the government list of candidates, made the following ominous forecast:

"We warn the people, we warn the government, that Kazakhstan is edging towards a situation preceding a civil war…Those who do not see this are criminally blind—and those who do not prevent this are criminally cowardly."

If Suleimenov's prediction were to come true, it would leave a huge vacuum of power, which China, Russia, or some other power would thirst to fill. The March 1994 elections will be the singular most important event to test Suleimenov's prediction.

◆   ◆   ◆

Nazarbayev Returns...Money in Hand

Nazarbayev returned to Kazakhstan from his trip to the U.S. For the 1994 fiscal year, Kazakhstan received $91 million in foreign aid. Clinton pledged $311 million for the 1995 fiscal year and an additional $80 for conversion of military facilities to civil use. Foreign assistance will provide Kazakhstan with an important stimulus for the economy, but it will not be a panacea for all of the ills of Kazakhstan. And handouts sometimes nurture a beggar's mentality. For example, I recently taught a course for business people. The business school charged the thirty students $110 each for the course and paid me and the other six teachers in the course less than $5 each. The teachers together received about $30 out of the proceeds of $3,330 from the students. I did not mind the exploitation. I am here to teach and the school gave me an audience; but my meeting with the rector of the school revealed the ugly side of a beggar's mentality. He requested a meeting with me, but his secretary did not tell me the purpose of the meeting. I went to his office. We exchanged observations on the educational system, and then he informed me that he needed legal representation in the U.S. in a commercial dispute with an American company, in which the amount in dispute was about $18,000. I gave him an idea of what lawyers charge. Without any embarrassment, he asked me whether any lawyers work for free. I was puzzled. What did he have in mind? "Well," he explained, "there are all these programs giving money to Kazakhstan; maybe there is an aid program to give free legal assistance to this institution." I informed him that I did not know of any, but he might want to try a contingency fee arrangement. No, he wanted a lawyer for free.

The people of Kazakhstan are not beggars, and aid programs should not presuppose that those who receive need not give anything in return. The recipients would only act like this rector. Kazakhstan must rely on its own strengths to survive in the post-Soviet era. During

World War II, Japanese prisoners of war constructed one of the most attractive buildings in Alma-Ata, the Academy of Sciences building. But the people of Kazakhstan did not learn how to construct these buildings for themselves. Now is the time for Kazakhstan to learn how to build for itself, and Americans are as good as any of the rest to teach them.

7

The Elections and the Road Home

March 1994

Dzhambul on a Clear Day

As part of my "Tour Kazakhstan," I went to Dzhambul, a city near the border with Uzbekistan. The south of Kazakhstan is populated with more Kazakhs than the north, and weather is considerably milder than the severe conditions of the north.

I was told that Dzhambul is polluted, but, because of economic conditions, the major contributors to that pollution were not in operation during my visit. Consequently, many people are out of work, but the environment is cleaner. In comparison with Almaty, Dzhambul seemed rather civilized. Indeed, the city seemed much cleaner than Almaty. It even had functioning street lights, and all of the trees in the center of town were well pruned. Garbage was not piling up. The exteriors of buildings looked maintained. (Some of the city's detractors say that the cleanliness is a function of the city administration's heavy hand.)

Taraz with Cockroaches

The old name of the city was Taraz. The best hotel in town is called the Taraz. My local hosts made arrangements for me to stay at the Taraz Hotel, which has a reputation for its cockroaches. Arriving in the hotel, I thought that I would not be disappointed. An attractive woman was trying to make her way into the lobby. She was obviously a prostitute and not welcome at the hotel. The guard dragged her in, hitting her several times, and said that he would call the police to pick her up. I had arrived at the Taraz Hotel in Dzhambul.

Fortunately, the hotel is under renovation, which must have scared away the cockroaches. No more prostitutes appeared. I was in a two-room suite which was well heated and had hot water. Of course, like all other hotels in Kazakhstan, there were no shower curtains, an innovation that has not hit the former Soviet Union. (Even major Party dachas where I have stayed did not have shower curtains. During one stay, I had a great shower, but no shower curtain, and so I drenched all my toiletries, including Band-Aids. The cleaning woman neatly laid out each Band-Aid separately on the edge of the bath tub to dry them out.) The Taraz provided unexpectedly pleasant accommodations.

Street scene in Dzhambul.

Feeling Like a White Person

At one of the three lectures, one of the students used a phrase that I had not heard. She initially asked about the poverty level in the U.S. and wanted to find out how much it would cost to live above the poverty level, "not necessarily to live like a white person." A "white person," I thought. I asked her about this phrase. She said that a "white person" is one who feels superior to others, someone who may have just received his or her salary. Even though she was an ethnic Kazakh, I learned that this expression enjoys popularity among both Kazakhs and Russians alike. Later on, when I was talking with a group of Russians, some told me that sometimes Russians use this expression in relation to Kazakhs. The expression appears to have its roots in Soviet propaganda, in relation to how the whites treated Native Americans in the U.S.

Challenges

The major challenge for universities is keeping the faculty intact. Faculty members routinely receive offers in the private sector or at other institutions for more money. One of the women who hosted me is committed to her work, and her students and colleagues respect this commitment. As a small measure of her devotion, she painted the halls and classrooms with the help of her students and with paint donated by local business people. Teachers with her devotion are few and far between.

Observations on the Elections

I had the opportunity to meet with some candidates in the upcoming regional and national elections. One candidate preferred to speak with me in Kazakh through a translator, even though he knew Russian. He did not seem to have any special platform, just broad support for reducing crime and providing for pensioners. Another candidate, Tauekekbek Zhanakulov, was running in the 48th Electoral District.

His campaign literature recalled his visit to Japan, where he studied the "Japanese miracle." He was "certain" that incorporating Japanese methods into the development of Kazakhstan would facilitate the material well-being of Kazakhstanis. I did not perceive that any of the candidates I met with were leading contenders.

The electorate is either apathetic or, more likely, skeptical about the elections. Many expect the turnout will be low. It has been hard to get the message out. The Election Commission has allowed candidates to print only 1000 copies of their platform. The candidates have been allotted ten minutes on television and ten minutes on radio. Media coverage has been minimal.

Fresno-Dzhambul: Sister Cities

Almukhan Isakov, the deputy head of the regional administration, agreed to meet with me. He was formerly the chairman of the Dzhambul Regional Soviet before it was dissolved. Before that, Isakov was the head of the Ideology Department for the Regional Committee of the Communist Party. Isakov offered his view that the electorate would not turn out in great numbers. According to Isakov, the people have "lost faith in reform." They have lived too long in chaotic conditions. The leaders in the Soviet Union made the same promises in 1989. But it is a matter of time. Said Isakov, "Even America wasn't born in one day."

In the Soviet era, a 98 percent turnout on election day was considered low, explained Isakov. This first democratic election may not even attract 50 percent of the voters in certain districts. Of the eight electoral districts within the Dzhambul Oblast, Isakov predicted that two or three would not have the requisite 50 percent of the registered votes to qualify the election results. He predicted a 65 percent Kazakh majority in parliament, but he agreed that the election was unpredictable.

Isakov was one of the founding members of the Rebirth of Kazakh Culture group, but he now believes that nationalism has gone out of vogue in the Dzhambul region. Kazakh nationalist organizations such as Alash, Azat, and Zheltoksan have very little support in the Dzhambul Region, according to Isakov. Even the Socialist Party has lost some of its appeal. The major party is SNEK, the Party of Unity of Kazakhstan.

Isakov said that, when he was a member of the Communist Party, he worked to minimize the differences between nationalities. Interestingly, Isakov credited this effort during the Soviet era with the high level of tolerance among nationalities today. He believed that two or three parties would emerge before the next parliamentary elections. These were the first elections. "Next time it will be better," concluded Isakov.

Isakov was eager to share his experience in Fresno, California. Isakov, like many Dzhambul residents, is proud of the city's relationship with Fresno. The Mayor of Fresno invited Isakov to Fresno. Isakov's week in Fresno had a major impact on Isakov's thinking. He was especially impressed by the work of the City Council of Fresno. The Fresno City Council has only nine members, compared to the City Supreme Soviet of Dzhambul, which had 100 members; and the Fresno City Council accomplishes twice as much work, according to Isakov.

There is a prominent sign on one of the main squares in Dzhambul where Communist Party slogans once were prominently displayed. It reads: "Dzhambul-Fresno: Sister Cities." There is a park named after Fresno, and several residents of Dzhambul have visited Fresno.

More Cultural Particularities

My hosts had me over for a bountiful dinner. The husband had started before the guest of honor had arrived. I was told that he was usually shy, but had "filled up" with a friend before dinner. Some American women have told me about aggressive men at the dinner table. Nevertheless, I was surprised as the host's husband said a toast and then tried to French kiss one of the other women at the table…in front of his own wife. Strange, but maybe not so strange. As strange as it may seem to us, old Kazakh tradition allowed a man to share his wife with a guest. In accordance with another tradition, because the steppe is flat and barren, a Kazakh would place a long stick in the ground if he wanted to have some "quality time" with his wife. Others would see the "urga" from a distance and not bother the couple.

And if you are over to a Kazakh's house, do not compliment anything, as it is the custom for the host to give guests anything that they admire. I knew this, but I had completely forgotten as I was shown a beautiful vase from India. I almost ended up with the vase, but I talked my way out of it.

Religion in Dzhambul

Religion is making a comeback in Kazakhstan. In Karaganda, a predominantly Russian city, there is a huge mosque under construction. In Dzhambul, a predominantly Kazakh city, a new Russian orthodox church is being built. Missionaries are in and around Dzhambul, teaching English. They serve an important role in educating locals in English but, of course, interweave a religious content in their lessons. The only man on the English faculty at the Pedagogical Institute told me in good English: "Yes, I believe in Jesus." A missionary with his children live in one of the villages around Dzhambul, learning local customs and the Kazakh language. According to some of my Kazakh friends who are enamored of the work of the missionaries, missionaries focus their efforts on Kazakhs, not Russians.

I went to the Karakhan Mausoleum, which, like other religious places, was turned into a museum during the Soviet era. The caretaker recites the daily prayers in the mausoleum. He was washing his arms and face outside the mausoleum as we approached him. He had a kind and soft voice and a youthful beard. He was probably in his early thirties. He showed us the outside of the mausoleum and then showed me another mausoleum about 100 meters away. Speaking through a woman Kazakh translator, he took great pride in telling me that the mausoleum was dedicated to a Moslem who had come and "vanquished" the Buddhists and others, claiming the right of the land for the Moslems. According to the caretaker, the only legitimate religion is Islam, and only devils on earth prevent others from embracing the religion.

He made it clear that there was little room for other religions in the area. He asked my opinion, and I told him that similar views had led to wars in other parts other world. He responded that, if that was Allah's will, so be it. In any event, we got along well, and, even though he originally resisted my request to see the inside of the mausoleum, he relented and showed me the inside. Since the translator was a woman, she was not allowed in the mausoleum. So it was just the two of us. We got along just fine, and we shifted to talking in Russian. We did not discuss the new huge Russian Orthodox Church under construction on the outskirts of the city.

◆   ◆   ◆

Housing Challenges...Again

I have moved again, settling into my new apartment in a prime location in the center of town on Gogol Street. Life in my new apartment is not without problems. One of the attractions of this apartment was the security. The entry door downstairs had a combination lock. There is only one problem: the lock was broken the day I moved in.

I share the apartment with these persistent, small, slow-moving moths. No matter how many I kill, they keep on reappearing. Another challenge is the lack of any hot water. In fact, there is no hot water throughout the entire city center. (In other preparations for the election, the traffic light workers are on strike, and many of the downtown traffic lights are not operating. And of course the garbage continues to pile up. Democracy in action!)

My new apartment (with me in it) suffers from poor heating. I never could understand why people would use their ovens for heating. It is really fantastic how much heat the oven can generate. Of course, if there were an interruption in the gas for any reason and someone wanted to light a cigarette, there would be quite a light show.

The cockroaches also like the heat. I had solved my cockroach problem in my last abode, but a new place, a new challenge. The critters like to sun themselves next to the oven. A friend suggested a pool and umbrellas for them.

◆   ◆   ◆

Travel Adventures Continue

"Tour Kazakhstan" took me to Semipalatinsk. Semipalatinsk is in the north, read cold! Since the price of my Intourist ticket was ten times the tenge rate, I had the pleasure of using the Intourist lounge. This time, the lounge was overflowing with local passengers bound for Germany. KazAir just bought a Boeing 747, which was used for Nazarbayev's visit to the U.S. When Nazarbayev is not traveling, the plane is used to fly the Germany route.

Most of the passengers were traveling to Germany in one direction. They are Germans from Kazakhstan who are immigrating to Germany. They have gathered their lives' possessions. Their friends and relatives see them off. A few minutes before their scheduled departure time, the announcement came. The plane was ready except for one problem: jet fuel. Come back tomorrow at noon, they were told.

Semipalatinsk

Landing in Semipalatinsk in a Soviet-built Yakovlev Yak-40, a small plane with a capacity of about 30 passengers, I saw what appeared to be Soviet fighter jets on the tarmac. Semipalatinsk was a closed city, and still outside the city is the nuclear testing site, the home of almost 500 nuclear detonations. Testing has been discontinued. Several huge smokestacks billow black smoke. I expected the worst.

Even though it was March, the pervasive cold is what I remember most about Semipalatinsk. It was only minus 15, a warming trend for those who live on the steppe, but not for this visitor. My room was heated, barely. The temperature in the room was in the forties. I spent much of the time with blankets wrapped around me. My visit to Semipalatinsk led me to the inescapable conclusion that I would not have fared well in a Stalinist camp.

Semipalatinsk is a city of exiles. The great poet Abai Kunanbaev, known simply as Abai, lived nearby. Dostoyevsky was exiled to Semipalatinsk. Semipalatinsk is a city with a history. The weather is severe, and the city is stark and grandiose. Nevertheless, those who live in Semipalatinsk take pride in their city.

The Irtysh Hotel and Lenin Square

The Irtysh river divides the city in two. I stayed at the Irtysh Hotel, overlooking the main square. Those readers who have been to any former Soviet city probably have an idea of the name of the square: Lenin Square. An imposing statue of Vladimir Lenin towers over the square. Forget subtlety, this is a huge statue, much larger than the one in Almaty. Those from Semipalatinsk laugh at the statue, because it looks like Lenin is waiting for his dance partner, his right arm raised to accept the arm of his partner. The statue of Abai is not far away, also of huge proportions, but somehow more subtle. Abai lived about 100 miles from Semipalatinsk, and the city is preparing for the 150th anniversary of his birth in 1995.

The nuclear testing site is still a part of the consciousness of the area, even though the last nuclear detonation was in 1989. One woman recalled how the tremors violently shook the city for four decades, rattling chandeliers and people's spirits. It was customary to drink 100 grams of vodka after each explosion, to calm one's nerves. The testing has ceased after 467 nuclear detonations, but the tradition continues.

Semipalatinsk is much more conservative than other cities in Kazakhstan. Friends still call each other "comrade." At meetings with candidates, the speaker in Moscow or Almaty might begin with the phrase: "Dear Friends"; in Semipalatinsk, he would say: "Comrades!" In Semipalatinsk, people speak warmly of their affiliation with the communist youth group.

But Semipalatinsk seemed clean. The kiosks that litter the streets in Almaty are not present in Semipalatinsk. The cold weather, however, does not deter the street merchants. People seemed friendlier and more hospitable than in Karaganda. But many of the Russians are leaving Semipalatinsk. At a dinner, a woman raised a toast to her city. She stood for her toast, "I will never leave my land. Many of my friends have left. My family is here. I was born here. I will never leave." Tears streamed down her cheeks.

Bakaleia: A New Kind of Store

A new company has opened several new stores. I was delighted to see these new stores. They differ in several major aspects from their state counterparts. The sales staff, all women, wear uniforms and are polite. If you go into a state store, you have to memorize all of the goods you want to buy, pay for those goods, then go back to the various counters with your receipt. You can only buy as much as your memory allows. In the Bakaleia stores, you pick up your goods and then go to the checkout stand.

Bakaleia has a meager selection. The bank at which Bakaleia kept its money on deposit froze the company's accounts for months, stripping the company of the cash it needed to stock its stores. Despite the setback, Bakaleia is on the move. It even uses one of its facilities to feed old pensioners in three shifts, 40 people in each shift. Bakaleia receives the names of the neediest pensioners in the region. And the meals are not the soup kitchen type of meals. They look, dare I say, appetizing. The pensioners sit around small tables for four or five people.

Most of the guests were old Russian women. There may be several explanations why the neediest are Russian women. Most were women because the life expectancy of men is as much as ten years shorter than for women. Also, this is the generation that lost an entire generation of men in World War II. My Kazakh hosts offered a couple of reasons for the prevalence of Russian women. Russian families have fewer children, who otherwise could take care of their elderly parents. Also, Kazakhs are supposed to take care of their parents at home, while this tradition is not as ingrained in Russian families.

The bread was tastier in Semipalatinsk than in Almaty, and the newly privatized restaurant in the center of town served five kinds of Moldavian wine along with a sumptuous meal. Although I suffered through the bitter cold, there were some amenities in Semipalatinsk.

On the Campaign Trail

I was invited to Semipalatinsk by Aitbai Konysbayev. Konysbayev, a former member of parliament who was running from his home district outside of Semipalatinsk. In 1991, Nazarbayev was asked to mediate the dispute between Armenia and Azerbaijan about Nagorno-Kara-bakh. Konysbayev was sent to the area as part of a delegation to negotiate a disengagement agreement. Six people from Kazakhstan were sent; four returned in coffins after a helicopter crash. Konysbayev was later elected to parliament by the Union of Lawyers.

The district in which Konysbayev is running is comprised of 78,000 eligible voters, 43 percent of whom are Russian; 34 percent, Kazakh; and 18 percent, German. Konysbayev has heavy competition from another former deputy, also a Kazakh. The former first secretary of the Obkom, the regional Communist Party, is also mounting a serious campaign. In the last days leading up to the election, Konysbayev, along with candidates for other offices, planned four or five meetings a day with voters. I was invited to attend some of these meetings.

Democracy in the Raw

Despite the shortcomings of the election process, the election has compelled candidates to take their campaigns to the people. The election is the first time candidates must seek support from a specific district. The impact of this accountability is diminished, however, when the winning candidates serve for five years, as provided for under the Constitution.

Konysbayev's district outside of Semipalatinsk is a rural area dominated by collective farms, which have now been transformed to collective enterprises. They survive primarily on their meat and dairy products industry. We visited the Semipalatinsk Collective Enterprise and the Talitsa Collective Enterprise.

Village outside of Semipalatinsk.

Semipalatinsk is a big city, mostly surrounded by steppe stretching endless miles. We took a two-lane road towards the collective farms. We passed the well-kept single family dwellings on the outskirts of town, with the "conveniences" outside of course. But then it was flat steppe covered with snow. There were some picturesque forests that were the site of youth camps in the summer. There was an occasional collective farm with a small population, generally no more than 3,000 to 4,000.

The candidates gave their stump speeches, but there was little enthusiasm in their voices after nonstop campaigning for two months.

Konysbayev talked about credit lines from the European Bank for Reconstruction and Development, not of great relevance to the lives of these collective farmers. Like the other candidates, Konysbayev was running on his biography, not any specific plan. Konysbayev did not tap any of his rich personal experience to humanize the campaign.

The candidates criticized self-nominated candidates. "They have to have money behind them," commented one speaker. Referring to the self-nominated candidates, another candidate implored the audience: "Don't let the *Mafioso* take seats in parliament." They also urged support for professionals, which apparently does not include one of Konysbayev's major opponents, a doctor. One speaker supporting Konysbayev added up the number of laws that Konysbayev's committee passed in the last parliament. Forget about whether any of these laws made any difference in the lives of Kazakhstanis; it is the number of laws that is the badge of honor. Another speaker supporting a candidate who grew up on a collective farm added, "No one understands the land like we understand the land. We need to support each other." No one made even a mention of the nationality question.

The candidates' stump speeches were long on words and statistics but short on what the candidates stood for. About 40 people attended each of the meetings and showed as much enthusiasm as one would at a funeral. It was painfully apparent that none of these candidates had run an election campaign. Where the candidate was educated and worked were of greater moment than what the candidate stood for. As one candidate aptly stated, "One hears the most lies before elections, during war, and after fishing."

Group gathers to hear the candidates in unheated room.

The question and answer period was opened with the following phrase, "Any questions, comrades?" And the audience, small and contained, was not interested in speeches. They wanted to know about what affected their lives. They wanted to know about prices. They wanted to know why their community bania had been closed down for five months. They wanted to know about the coal supply. They wanted to know about the pensions they have not received for four months. One elderly woman captured the entire spirit of the election. She was a member of the collective farm. She rose out of her seat and, in a clear and simple voice, told the candidates: "We don't need anything from you. We just want to get our pensions."

Election Apathy among Students

I gave a lecture at the Technology Institute, and during the question and answer period I had a chance to ask the students whether they would vote. Not surprisingly, most did not seem interested in the election. One student simply told me that he would vote for whomever his parents told him to vote for. Traditional respect for one's elders takes on a new meaning in Semipalatinsk. Another student opined that these were random candidates: "We aren't expecting much."

Return Travel Arrangements

Kazakhstan Airlines charges foreigners a dollar price. The price of a ticket to Semipalatinsk costs 120 tenge, or less than $10. For foreigners, the price is $102. At 4:00 PM I arrived an hour early for registration for my return flight to Almaty, only to learn that my flight had been delayed at least until 8:00 PM. Translation: I would be lucky to leave Semipalatinsk. There are several flights a day. The passengers on the early morning flight to Almaty still had not left, but their plane, a Yakovlev Yak-40 with a seating capacity of about 30 passengers, was readying for departure. My hosts quickly prevailed on the airport administration for me to board the flight. I do not know if someone was removed from the flight, and I suppose that I would feel guiltier if I had not paid more than ten times the fare as locals.

The two-hour flight went smoothly. Almaty was cold again, barely above zero. The Boeing was still at the airport in Almaty. I do not know whether it flew this past week at all. More importantly for my circumstances, the bus to take passengers from the plane to the terminal was nowhere to be seen. Of course, the flight attendants let everyone off the plane. We waited in the bitter cold, for five minutes, then ten minutes. The flight attendants yelled at anyone who wanted to walk the 300 yards to the terminal to wait. We waited some more. One bus went right by us. A supply truck came up to supply another plane with tonic water. I joked that at least we could drink the tonic water while we waited. Then the passengers revolted. We all bolted to the terminal across the tarmac. So much for Soviet-style discipline.

◆　　　◆　　　◆

Final Observation on Elections

Nazarbayev said he wanted a professional parliament, although it was not clear what constituted professionalism. Was it a standing parliament, or people with a certain background? Should cosmonauts and doctors be disqualified, to let lawyers and economists run the show? Tokhtar Aubakirov, the first Kazakh cosmonaut, was running in a district outside of Karaganda. One candidate asked: "We have few qualified people. Aubakirov is the most qualified we have in his field. Why is he running for parliament?"

Disaffection runs high. On my way back to Almaty, I met a young woman, Toleuzhamal, from Semipalatinsk. Her voice summarized the views of the vast majority of others I met these past several weeks. As she said: "I am not going to vote. I don't believe in the elections. There are too many candidates. The self-nominated candidates are only doing it for their own good. If I knew someone, I would vote for them. Just too many words and little action."

The candidates have not been able to get their message out. The result is that the electorate is utterly uninformed on the issues, has no idea of who to vote for, and does not have the means to find out. Every candidate theoretically has the same chance, armed with a paltry $400 to spend. They exhausted these funds on a few posters and a few minutes on radio and television. There has been virtually no grassroots effort. There is barely a trace of campaign activity. Posters of the White Brotherhood, a cult group based in Ukraine, have more of a presence in Almaty than campaign posters. I have seen two, that's right, all of two banners promoting a candidate in the entire city of Almaty. There have been no rallies or debates. Newspapers were in mysteriously short supply. I could not find a newspaper in Almaty for most of the week. All in all, the campaign has been a very staid affair. People have very little clue of the candidates they are supporting.

Nazarbayev, possibly sensing the skepticism, made an impassioned plea on television to get out the vote. It was Nazarbayev at his best, as he stared into the camera, entreating his fellow citizens:

"[E]very Kazakhstani, as citizens of one state, in every sphere of life, has one common global interest, which is why they constitute a single ethno-political community. Every person is above all a citizen of this land, and then a Kazakh, Russian, Ukrainian, German, or someone else....Fellow countrymen, the progress and democratic development of our republic depends on your participation and views, on your sound and weighty choice...We are going to the first democratic elections in the history of Kazakhstan. Without exaggeration, the whole world is watching...."

All that remains are the elections. Kazakhstan awaits the judgment of its people to determine whether democracy can take hold on the steppe of Central Asia.

◆   ◆   ◆

The Day of the Elections

Some traditions die hard. Along with the elections, *ad hoc* stores opened up, selling quality products at reduced prices at voting stations. The ballots for the three elections—for city, regional and national elections—would look strange to a foreigner. As under Soviet practice, the voter crosses off the names of the candidates for whom he or she does not want to vote. In the old days, this process meant that it was quicker to vote because there was only one candidate. The voter would come, and many came on behalf of other members of his or her family, to pick up the ballots and put them into the voting box. He did not need to do anything.

The area around the voting precincts was supposed to be cleared of campaign posters. There was a moratorium on campaigning the day before the election. The election commissions had removed the campaign literature before the election. But, as I arrived in the morning, these posters had appeared again; and why not? There was no sanction for getting your candidate's name out in front of the voters.

A Shadow Vote

A friend told me that I could be her shadow vote. She would vote for whomever I told her. So I tried to gather information about my candidates, but there wasn't any information. One local newspaper had asked several questions of candidates, but probably only a third had participated in the survey. Many of the candidates in my district refused to reply to the questions. For local candidates running for the local councils, now known as "*maslikhats*," there was no information.

I still had not made up my mind when I arrived for voting. There were a few campaign posters still up, which I read along with others going into the voting booths. These were supposed to have been removed, but they were the only source of information. After a few moments of reading the poster, one young man turned away and exclaimed, "Let's get on with voting. What's the difference?" It was clear that this was not an informed electorate.

The only source of information other than the newspaper survey was what was on the posters outside the precinct and the information on the ballot, which showed the party affiliation, if any (many were self-nominated), and profession of the candidate. I did what many others did, basing my decision on the candidate's party affiliation and profession. I joined the ranks of the uninformed voters. My friend crossed out the names of those we chose not to vote for.

Outside the precincts, I asked several voters why they voted the way they had. No one had any information about their candidates. They made up their mind based on the profession of the candidates. One elderly woman criticized a doctor for running. "What business does a doctor have in parliament?" she asked rhetorically. A young Russian man was quite clear: "I used one main criterion: whether they were Russian. You can feel the struggle for power, and I wanted to vote for my own." Another person informed me that she used solely the candidates' biographies and educational background on which to base her vote. The voters had no basis on which to make an informed decision.

I spoke with the head of a local election commission at one of the voting stations. As of late morning, only 500 of the 2,500 registered voters in his district had voted. Most activity in the precincts occurred in the morning. Remember, 50 percent of registered voters were required to constitute the election as valid. Apparently the word went out in early afternoon to some areas to get out the vote. Representatives of the election commissions started their campaign to get out the vote, going door to door with portable voting boxes. It is not clear the extent to which this activity affected the results, but this activity showed a flagrant disregard of the election procedure.

International Women's Day or the Day after the Elections

March 8th is International Women's Day. In the Soviet era, men would do the housework for a day, cook, and do other household chores. Although it is "international," it is not on my Hallmark calendar. People here are very surprised to learn that the West does not celebrate this holiday. More importantly, it is the day after the first "democratic" elections in Kazakhstan. I heard that preliminary figures showed that voter turnout was 72 percent, a rate of participation that far surpassed all indications that I and others had.

"The Goal of Fair and Free Elections Was Not Reached"

This was the pronouncement of the head of the delegation representing the Parliamentary Assembly of the Conference on Security and Cooperation in Europe. There were, in his words, "serious shortcomings," including short notice of the election, the presidential list, confusing ballot system, and registration of candidates, among several others. The most serious problem was the turnout. My own anecdotal information and the observations of international observers contradicted the preliminary estimate of the Election Commission that 72 percent of the electorate voted. There was a strange double standard: when the candidates were required to gather petitions, they had to gather signatures from 3,000 people. One person could not sign for other members of his or her family. On election day, people with passports of several members of their family came to the polls to vote for themselves and several members of their family. The CSCE estimated that as many as 35 to 50 percent of the vote was cast in this manner.

The opinion of the various international observer groups was unanimous. Now it is for the president to determine what to do. There are some who believe that the president should annul the results. The reaction of the international community will be critical. The election commission will have to review the results, and it is their decision whether to modify the results in individual districts.

The news conference of the international observers was full of intrigue. The CSCE took the lead with a diplomatic but clear message. One U.S. observer exclaimed, "I would not want to defend these elections in court." The news conference received little attention in the domestic press, but the international media were there. The commercial stations gave some attention to the findings, but I could not find any coverage by the state press.

The evening of the news conference, a reception was held for two strange bedfellows: the Central Election Commission and the 124 international observers, who had just panned the election process. The atmosphere was awkward. The Deputy Minister of Foreign Affairs, Viacheslav Guizzatov, a frequent visitor at the Embassy, was livid and cornered the U.S. ambassador. The ambassador has worked incredibly hard to develop good relations between the U.S. and Kazakhstan, and the elections would undoubtedly put a damper on this developing relationship. In conversations with members of the Election Commission at the reception, I was told that they had not received warning of the news conference or been given an opportunity to respond.

Despite the methodology of the election, the new parliament will more accurately reflect the ethnic mix in the country, a stride towards democracy. Preliminary information was that 55 percent of the new parliament will be Kazakh; 45 percent, non-Kazakh. This figure might change. The government will have some difficult decisions about whether to endorse the elections.

One Disappointed Candidate

And the controversy about the international observers got hotter and hotter. On the independent commercial station, there was considerable coverage. On the state station, there was hardly a mention of the elections. There would not be many appeals. As one disappointed candidate told me: "Appeals are for the weak." The Central Election Commission held a press conference. The head of the Commission declared that the elections had been "successful," although there were few voters who would subscribe to this view.

President Nazarbayev went on television to dismiss the results of the international observers. Nazarbayev said that several members of CSCE did not agree with the findings and that these were the best democratic elections "under the circumstances."

◆   ◆   ◆

Bania and the End of Ramadan

The winter of 1993–1994 was the coldest in years. I spoke with one veteran of 46 winters in Almaty. Never has it been so cold for so long in Almaty. But spring has sprung in Almaty, finally. It reached the fifties, almost warm, but an inch of ice has remained on the sidewalks. After an interruption in supplies for several months, juice again appeared in the kiosks. But there has been no problem obtaining vodka in the past several months. Today it is raining, creating treacherous conditions on the roads and walkways. But it is spring in Almaty!

Trying to manage the sidewalks, I slipped several times. The disabled and elderly had to make a Herculean effort to make it even a few blocks. There are no wheelchair access sidewalks or buildings. Many amputees walk on crutches. How they muster enough strength to cope with these conditions is beyond imagination.

To minimize the risk of combating the elements, I decided to stay at home and work, but the phone rang, derailing my plans. I was summoned for another excursion to Arasan, the magnificent baths. My hosts were those with whom you may already be familiar: Didenko, my friend and colleague on the law faculty; Raev, former people's deputy on the human rights committee; and Konysbayev, also a former deputy. Raev and Konysbayev just completed their campaigns for the new parliament. Both campaigned hard and lost.

At the baths, despite their losses, Raev and Konysbayev were relaxed, and neither expressed any bitterness. Both were drained by the campaign. Konysbayev ran third in his race. Raev lost by just a couple of hundred of votes. At first blush, Konysbayev and Raev are strange friends. Their views differ on virtually everything. But there is a part of their common history that binds them together as brothers. In 1991, Konysbayev and Raev were sent as emissaries along with four comrades to Nagorno-Karabakh, an Armenian enclave in the middle of Azerbaijan. Their mission was to help mediate the violent dispute between Armenia and Azerbaijan. Their four colleagues were killed in a helicopter crash. Raev and Konysbayev frequently spend time together, remembering their colleagues.

In the baths, we spent more time talking and drinking than sweating. Konysbayev drafted his son, Baurzhan, who has a car, to pick us up after the baths and serve as our designated driver for the rest of the day. Baurzhan is a law student, who enjoys the rare privilege of having a car. It was apparent that Baurzhan had other things to do. He is a handsome young man, speaks good English, and works for a Western accounting firm. He was wearing a new leather jacket, which cost him $280. He was not dressed to take four old guys around, but he did not register his dissatisfaction, saying nothing in accordance with the "Eastern way," as Konysbayev pointed out. Raev insisted on speaking

Kazakh with Baurzhan, for what appeared to be my benefit. Baurzhan understood but responded in Russian, obviously frustrating Raev. The road will be long to reestablish the primacy of Kazakh as the language of Kazakhstan.

◆　　◆　　◆

Will Taxes Cure the Ills of Kazakhstan?

Most Kazakhstanis avoid taxes, not really evading them, because very few pay taxes. Rather than enforcing existing tax laws, the president decided to impose a graduated tax system. For individuals earning more than $100, the tax rate will be 60 percent. With as many as twenty different kinds of taxes, it is no wonder that few understand the taxes, and most simply ignore them. Consequently, it will not affect most Kazakhstanis, but it will affect the few honest foreigners and Kazakhstanis who pay their taxes. One thing is for sure: the new tax rate will add little to government coffers and will not be a solution for the ills of Kazakhstan.

Who Will Lead This Country?

Can the new legislature make inroads on the challenges facing the country? Next month, in April 1994, the new legislature will be convened. The elections through which this legislature was elected are still the subject of considerable controversy. There are hundreds of appeals, which will keep the Central Election Commission busy for a while. Nazarbayev virtually ignored the criticism that the European Parliament leveled at Kazakhstan. But nobody believes that 75 percent of the electorate went to the polls. As one election official told me, "In any event, if we had to run the elections again, it would be too costly." I replied that lack of funds would probably not pass the red face test as a sufficient reason for not having fair elections.

The parliament is officially slated to remain in office for five years, although many believe that it will suffer the fate of the last parliament: early retirement.

We have some idea of what the new parliament will look like, if one can believe the stated positions of the candidates before the candidates were elected. One poll elicited the views of about 38 percent of candidates who eventually won seats in the new parliament. Of the candidates who gave responses and who will be in the next parliament, 57 percent were in favor of private ownership of land; 43 percent against. The responses among Kazakhs and non-Kazakhs were roughly the same.

Regarding Russian as a state language, 61 percent are for it; 39 percent against. But these data were skewed, because more Russians were included in the survey. The Kazakh and non-Kazakh members of the new parliament will be sharply divided on this issue. Only 35 percent of the Kazakhs who gave responses and who will be in the next parliament are for Russian as a state language. In sharp contrast, 86 percent of the Russians who responded and who will be in the next parliament are for Russian as a state language.

And the Final Assessment of the New Parliament Is…

If you believe the survey, what was unthinkable a year ago, may become law: private ownership of land. But the issue of Russian as a state language will be extremely divisive in the new parliament. Based on the results, there will be a majority in favor of Russian as a state language but far less than two-thirds of the parliament necessary to amend the Constitution. Without strong presidential support, this parliament will not widely support Russian as a state language. Despite the problems associated with the election, this parliament may be much more independent than past parliaments. Half of the new parliament is not tied to any party or to the president, and there may be some strong divergence of views between the new parliament and the president.

The strength of the budding democracy in Kazakhstan may depend on how these differences will be resolved.

◆   ◆   ◆

No Neat Endings

I was hoping for a crisp, neat ending to my stay in Kazakhstan, on how democracy has found its way to the hinterlands. There were several hints of democracy. But the kind of neat ending for which I was hoping possibly occurs only in works of fiction. This country has immense potential, but democratic traditions have not yet been firmly implanted on the steppe of Central Asia. Like most nonfiction, there is no end, just the prologue to another book.

The Return of Kunaev

Kazakhstan will continue to struggle with its past as it builds its future. What many remember about the Soviet era is not the oppression of being a colony of Moscow, but the clean streets, the lack of crime, the stability and simplicity of Kazakhstan under Kunaev. I do not think that there is any serious movement to return to that era. The quest in this country is to balance the stability of the past with the freedoms—and chaos, under the new political order. Kazakhstanis understandably idealize the past, as they are uncertain about the future.

After Kunaev was removed in 1986, Soviet party officials blasted Kunaev "for crude violations of the norms of Party life, the creation of his personality cult...which led to the development in the republic of...abuses of official position, bribery, and corruption." Even Nazarbayev in 1987 reportedly blamed the "negative phenomena of the past few years" on "a quarter of a century the Party organization was headed by Dinmukhamed Kunaev." But the country has made a full turn and celebrates Kunaev's memory, as it longs to recapture the stability of Kunaev's tenure. Kunaev has withstood the test of time. Even though Kunaev died in August 1993, his influence will live on. There is no better indication of this influence as the recent renaming of Karl Marx Street. It will now be known as Kunaev Street.

◆   ◆   ◆

Helga and the Massage

My unaccommodating living conditions prompted me to flee to the mountains and a sanitarium, a health resort of sorts, for my last weekend in Kazakhstan. The sanitarium is reserved for the Ministry of Energy and stays are "limited" to a minimum of 10 days. They have not yet thought of weekend getaways. Nevertheless, I struck a bargain with the "chief doctor," the administrator of the sanitarium, to stay at the sanitarium for the weekend.

There was not much to do at the sanitarium except to eat and walk around. The disco consisted of loud music and about ten people in a circle gyrating back and forth. I have not a clue what people do for ten days at the facility.

When I was offered a massage, I readily accepted, thinking of the mud baths and massages of Calistoga, California. Instead I got Helga from hell (not her real name), who must have worked in the Stalinist camps in her former life. I was thinking of relaxation; she was thinking of therapy (a euphemism for torture, I am sure). She found every pressure point on my back until I was writhing in pain. Enough was enough after 36 minutes (not that I was counting the time). I passed on the massage on the second day of my visit.

Nauryz—Time of Renewal

When I returned to Almaty, I was caught unaware by yet another new holiday. Nauryz is a traditional Moslem holiday celebrating the New Year. It is not necessarily a religious holiday. The Soviets banned celebration of Nauryz in 1926, but in the post-Soviet era Nauryz has made a comeback. Nauryz has been an official state holiday since 1992. It is celebrated on March 22.

Crowds celebrate Nauryz.

Festivity was in the air, as dozens of yurts were set up on Panfilov Street. Even the foot of Lenin's statue got a yurt. Children were given rides on camels. Hot air balloons and skydivers highlighted the festivities. It was the first holiday since I arrived for which there was much of a hint of a genuine festive spirit.

Lenin and a yurt on Nauryz.

Almaty in Dire Need of Help

As I am preparing to leave, spring is finally settling in. And the traffic light engineers have not been paid in a couple of months. Traffic lights are not synchronized in Kazakhstan; in fact, they don't even work now. In the Soviet days, it wouldn't make any difference, for few had cars, but not anymore. Chaos reigns on the streets.

The snow has all but melted in Almaty. The thaw has revealed the decrepit infrastructure from years of neglect. Throughout town, there are potholes that would swallow a horse, or a car. According to my driver, "at least in Kunaev's time, I knew every pothole in town, and they were filled immediately. It was a hundred times better."

Garbage is again multiplying like maggots. The point is that with little effort the lives of so many could be vastly improved. Many Kazakhstanis who travel abroad bring back the message to their countrymen. We do not need to take this anymore. Unfortunately, few Kazakhstanis have traveled abroad, and many of those who have been abroad travel in only one direction. The Germans who could add so much to this country are leaving en masse. The Jewish population has left. And many in the Russian community have their bags packed. Those who stay have the great challenge of building a new country.

A Farewell from the City

Just in case I had any hesitation about leaving, the city presented me with several going away gifts. The phone was turned off. There was no hot water, again. I had some very, very cold showers. And the sink started leaking profusely, spilling water all over the kitchen floor. It was time to wash the dishes in the bathtub, with cold water. Any doubts about leaving were set to rest.

◆　　　◆　　　◆

What It Would Be Like to Be at Your Own Funeral

I hosted a party to bid farewell to my friends. A friend who works for the Embassy and lives in a palatial apartment lent his place for the festivities. The party was just a small token of my appreciation for those who injected meaning into my visit. There was plenty of booze: vodka for the locals and wine for the few Americans. But it was a party of local spirit, the reason that, despite all of the challenges, my visit had special meaning and purpose. The people who came to the party were the people who are building a new country in this vast unknown area somewhere to the left of China and to the right of the Caspian Sea.

These were my friends, friends that will likely bring me back to this part of the world. A couple of friends from the Embassy's information service came. Their mission sounds simple: bring accurate information to this area, where rumor and innuendo sometimes are the best source of news. Not only were they good friends, but they eased the burden of dealing with the hurly-burly of Almaty life.

Another friend was on the Central Election Committee. I lost track of how many times we went to the bania, sharing our views on politics and the elections. Raev and Konysbayev, now both former parliamentarians, were there. Both ran unsuccessful campaigns. One will go into business and make some money; despite our vast divergence of views, the country probably lost a valuable independent thinker. The other lost his race by two hundred votes. He will likely return to politics.

There was a contingent of law professors, including the father of civil law in Kazakhstan, Yuri Basin; the dean of the law school, Anatoli Matiukhin; and of course my good friend Anatoli Didenko. Having worked in anonymity for decades, now they are not only training, but guiding a new generation of attorneys.

William Courtney, the U.S. Ambassador who set up the Embassy in a hotel room in 1992, came to the gathering. He has been the messenger of some U.S. criticism of the government's policies. But the Kazakhstani government should appreciate that they probably could not have a more hardworking and devoted diplomat. He is a good friend of Kazakhstan and has a profound understanding of events in the former Soviet Union. He has tirelessly worked to further the relations between the U.S. and Kazakhstan.

There were other friends who came, who in their small and not so small way are building this country, the structures in this country that will survive after we are all long gone. The party assumed a local flavor. Everyone made a toast. There were 18 guests and, yes, 18 toasts, after which I would say the last toast, and everyone would go home. An authentic local party would have had the beshbarmak with the sheep's head. I had control of the menu. I passed on the beshbarmak. Anatoli Didenko, who has graced many of these pages many a time, served as the *talmada*, the master of ceremonies. Little did I know that he would turn the party into an evening of toasts to some of my adventures in the country. With a penchant for exaggeration, he was eloquent in toasting me. The rest of the toasts were of a similar ilk. It sounded like they were sermonizing a departed soul at a memorial service. I, of course, interrupted several times to remind all present that I was still alive and well and planned on that course of action for some time to come.

◆　　◆　　◆

On the Way Home

I bid farewell to Kazakhstan as I boarded a Soviet-built Ilyushin Il-86 bound for Frankfurt. The plane was filled to the gills with ethnic Germans bound for their "homeland" from which their ancestors emigrated two hundred years ago. In 1989, there were almost one million Germans living on the territory of Kazakhstan. Most speak better Kazakh than German.

Lenient immigration policies have encouraged the Germans to leave in hordes. As many as 300,000 (over 30 percent) of the German population has already left Kazakhstan, and, with flights three times a week from Dzhambul and another five from Almaty to Germany, most of which are filled, within a few years there will be few Germans left in Kazakhstan.

Musical Chairs—Bardak

Bardak is the Russian slang for pathetic disorder. (Remember this word, for its force pervades every aspect of Kazakhstani life.) For these departing Germans on board, they had to endure just a few more examples of *bardak* on the last days of their checkered history in Central Asia.

The route to Germany is now serviced by a Boeing, but, when the president flies abroad, he uses the plane, and a Soviet-built Il-86 makes the seven-hour trip from Almaty to Frankfurt. The plane has been remodeled and is roomy for its capacity of 234 passengers in two classes. The problem, as before, is fuel. The flight to Germany flew at half capacity because there was not enough fuel for the plane's entire capacity, stranding 100 passengers, mostly all emigrants. The stranded passengers were transferred to today's flight; but the major challenge for the émigrés on their last day in Kazakhstan was where to sleep while they waited. More than a hundred people, including small children and the elderly, slept on their life's belongings…in the terminal. I learned that there were some who had actually spent three days at the airport!

The principle of bardak means that the airport personnel assured everyone left stranded by yesterday's flight that they would get on today, not knowing of course whether they were correct. I arrived at the airport just in time to see the aftermath of the announcement that everyone would not get on today's flights. Tempers were running very high.

The principle of bardak means that they let more people on the plane than there were seats, without counting how many passengers were already on the plane. An open seating policy means that more people than there were seats were able to get on the plane. Like in musical chairs, the odd person out would have to leave. Some desperate souls found an empty seat and put their children on their laps, not babies, but children, like a ten-year-old boy one row in front of me. For them, it would not be the most comfortable seven-hour flight, but better than the alternative: return to the terminal for another long wait. One lady brought her puppy onboard. Fortunately, there were no chickens or other farm animals.

The principle of bardak means that maintenance is low on these planes. I was just a little ill at ease as we were taking off. The runway is very long, and we seemed to need every bit of it. We were not going very fast and the planes' wheels were still firmly on the runway. With the maximum passengers aboard, and cargo compartments filled, we were probably loaded to the limit. We seemed to labor on the runway, trying to take off for a long, long time. I thought that we would soon find ourselves on the fields. But we finally pulled off the ground. I looked at the fields below the plane. We probably had less than 100 yards to spare.

There is no excuse for the disorder at the airport or on the streets. Bardak exacts a toll, not only on the sterile statistics of the gross domestic product, but also more importantly on people's sense of well-being.

The flight crew forgot to grab a video. (An innovation on flights in the former Soviet Union—but they don't have headphones; they just blast all the passengers with the voice track.) One of the passengers lent an American sex and violence film, with views of women getting raped, taking showers, etc. It was interesting entertainment for this plane filled with German émigrés.

The Sins of Living in Kazakhstan

The man sitting next to me was an affable ethnic German, Sasha, who was leaving Kazakhstan with his second wife. Sasha's wife was noticeably pregnant. They were leaving with their three children (the eldest child is from his wife's first marriage). He is a practicing Baptist. With little prompting, Sasha eagerly confessed his sins: illegal payments to facilitate his departure.

Sasha explained Germans have worked hard to earn money, but, now that they are leaving, the locals believe that the Germans should share their wealth and leave with very little in their pockets. Sasha complained that he had no choice but to pay bribe after bribe. Every bureaucrat can hinder the emigration process. It is now part of the ritual that those Germans leaving pay a kind of bounty. Sasha enumerated the long process, first of getting the invitation from Germany, taking as long as a couple of years, and then jumping through the several hoops of getting the right paperwork in order. The problems with the paperwork are readily cured with some money. With money directed into the right hands, Germans can leave within a couple of months after receiving the official invitation.

At the airport, the bureaucrats have a useful tool to determine how much to demand from the helpless émigrés. The émigrés, like all leaving the country, fill out customs slips showing the amount of hard currency that the departing passenger is taking. The émigrés' ability to pay is a useful measure for the bureaucrat. The amounts generally are not huge, but, with the average salary of the airport workers at the equivalent of $20, the incentive to demand money from the émigrés is great.

Sasha explained that these illegal payments exacted a heavy psychological toll on him, a kind of parting shot from the authorities. He described how crude these payments were. If he offered too little, the bureaucrat told Sasha that it might still be a long time to complete the process. The natural father of Sasha's stepdaughter wrote a letter to the authorities, protesting her departure to Germany; but there was one minor problem. The name of the purported father was misspelled. Nevertheless, Sasha had to pay the bounty.

Sasha conceded that the Germans have been well treated since they were deported en masse from the Volga in 1941. Most are leaving not because of overt discrimination, but rather because of a desire to improve their economic lot. Nevertheless, even a noticeable increase in the standard of living in Kazakhstan will do little to deter the mass exodus of Germans.

Let Stability Reign

In this part of the world, there will undoubtedly be further large population migrations; and, in contrast to the German migration from Kazakhstan, hate, prejudice, and bigotry will be the motivating factors. Kazakhstan is trying mightily to avoid this eventuality. It is attempting to create a stable home for those who want to stay and build a new country and to live peacefully with neighboring countries. President Nazarbayev has sent a clear, unambiguous, and powerful message that Kazakhstan is for all ethnic groups. Unlike leaders in other republics, he has tried to sculpt from the past an identity of tolerance for the country. In his words,

"There were unpleasant historical incidents—colonization, the Bolshevik regime and totalitarianism, when there was a purposeful process of denationalization of Kazakhs. But for this, Russia and the Russian people are not guilty. Those guilty were the oppressive Tsarist regime and the repressive Soviet system, from which the Russians themselves and others suffered no less. And there is something else that cannot ever be forgotten. In a difficult time, when the Kazakh people were threatened with complete annihilation, our ancestors turned to Russia and found their protector. In our grateful memory must always be preserved that Russia opened wide for us the doors of academic and scientific institutions, assisted in creating an industrial basis for the economy. Its best people devoted much effort to the formation of Kazakh culture...[A]greement and friendship among our peoples have their roots in the inherent Kazakh ability to live in good relations with representatives of any nation or people, in its great religious tolerance, [and in its] natural good will and deep respect of the interests of our neighbors."

The hurdles are enormous to Nazarbayev realizing his vision of interethnic harmony. The skyrocketing crime, the bureaucratic bungling, the graft, all threaten to derail the good intentions of Nazarbayev and like-minded politicians. Nevertheless, Kazakhstan has glimpsed the beacon of stability in the otherwise turbulent seas of Central Asia.

The stakes are high not only for the people who live in Kazakhstan, but also for those across its borders.

Stoic on Arrival

Arriving in Frankfurt, I scanned the faces of the German émigrés on the plane. They did not applaud and indeed showed little if any emotion. Were they sorry to leave their countries? Were they overcome by emotion? Their expressions showed none of these emotions. Maybe they were exhausted from generations separated from their homeland.

But there was at least one passenger who was not stoic. I have been out of the U.S. for many months and probably showed more emotion on my face than those arriving in Germany to their new homes. I probably showed some of the delight in the prospect of returning home. But even for me, there were hints of melancholy; despite the challenges of living in Kazakhstan, it has been an experience that has profoundly affected my life and has been wonderfully gratifying. I hope that, through these pages, you have attained a sense of not only the frustrations of life in Kazakhstan, but also the exhilaration of watching a new country emerge.

Epilogue

I was in Paris a few years back, taking a walk on the Left Bank of the Seine. I wandered into the renowned Shakespeare and Company bookstore, "the largest stock of antiquarian English books on the Continent." In a dusty shelf in the basement, one book caught my eye, and it wasn't in English. It was a Russian language book by Nursultan Nazarbayev entitled *On the Threshold of the 21st Century*, published in 1996. In his revealing book, Nazarbayev describes his version of some of the significant events of the early days of independence, which I had witnessed.

Nazarbayev recounts how he wanted to stay in the ruble zone and received assurances from Russian Prime Minister Viktor Chernomyrdin that Kazakhstan would be allowed to stay in a unified ruble zone with Russia. According to Nazarbayev's account, despite several assurances, on October 26, 1993, he learned from a Russian official that "the Russian train was leaving" without Kazakhstan. Nazarbayev had hoped that Russia would "not want to sever our economic relations in an hour." He conceded that he was wrong when he "believed, and therefore was convinced that friendly, economically strong Russia needed Kazakhstan as a strategic partner."

He quickly put into motion contingency plans to release the Kazakhstani currency, the tenge, which Nazarbayev had ordered printed in secret in Great Britain. Kazakhstan hired four Ilyushin Il-76 aircraft. In one week, these planes made 18 round-trips between London and Uralsk, carrying literally planeloads of the new money. And the tenge was released on November 12, 1993.

Nazarbayev's reminiscences of the nascent years of independent Kazakhstan are a good complement to what I observed and wrote about in the Almaty Journal. And Nazarbayev is right when he observes that those years represented a unique period in the formation of statehood of Kazakhstan. Nazarbayev concludes that "Now we can concentrate our efforts on the development of economic reforms and democracy. The revival of Kazakhstan statehood is the foundation on which democracy and a market economy can be built." Despite this prognostication, the progress towards democracy and a market economy has been marked by fits and starts, as I have witnessed in more than 15 trips back to Kazakhstan over the past years.

The trajectory of the country was set during the time that I wrote the Almaty Journal in 1993 and 1994. The country has developed, and yet it has stayed the same. The trips never ceased to amaze, inspire, and disappoint. I have felt on many occasions that I was coming home. On one of my visits, at the airport, a young Kazakh man came up to me, "Keet, good to see you." I looked at him intently, trying to discern where I knew him from. I don't think he was one of my students from my teaching days. Did I meet him at a party or was he at one of my lectures? I will never know. We exchanged pleasantries, but our brief conversation did not shed any light on how we were acquainted. But I was coming back to familiar territory. For all its faults, Kazakhstan is a place you can get your arms around.

Mud in My Face

One of my assessments that went wildly awry was to predict that the capital would not be moved from Almaty to the cold and barren wasteland of northern Kazakhstan. When Nazarbayev floated a trial balloon on moving the capital from Almaty to Akmola (formerly Tselinograd), I was skeptical. Why move the capital from the most beautiful and developed city in Kazakhstan to Akmola, which is planted right in the center of some of the bleakest and unforgiving terrain in Central Asia? Almaty in Kazakh means "father of apples"; Akmola means "white grave" (although some Kazakhs dispute this translation). I did not think I was going very far out on a limb with my prediction that the capital would not be moved. Guess what was announced during one of my visits to Almaty?

And indeed, in December 1997, Akmola was officially declared the new capital of Kazakhstan. The government voted to move the capital to Akmola. For those who did not like the Western translation of Akmola meaning "white tomb," which was fodder for much joking in the Western press, Nazarbayev issued a decree in 1998, changing the name of Akmola to Astana. Astana simply means "capital" in Kazakh. On June 10, 1998, the official opening of the new capital was held. A Western reporter for the *International Herald Tribune* described the festivities: "Redolent of North Korea's set-piece drill extravaganzas, it saw thousands of marchers in colored outfits hold up colored squares to form a vast tableau melding from Mr. Nazarbayev's portrait to a 'No Smoking' sign'…"

Shalom Has No Shalom

One of the places I went to a few times when I lived in Kazakhstan was the "Jewish restaurant," Shalom. During one of my meals, a man with his two bodyguards and their automatic weapons came in for an evening snack. The Shalom has closed; from what I heard, the owner's son was killed. The owner moved to Israel.

But not all has gone poorly for the Jewish community in Almaty. Jewish life has been reinvigorated with the opening of a Jewish Community Center, replete with classrooms, library, and soup kitchen for the poor. And there is a permanent synagogue.

The other religious communities have also seen a revival, not the least of which is the Moslem community. The new central mosque in Almaty, which was opened in 1999, can accommodate up to 3,000 worshippers. The dome is more than 100 feet high and the minaret, dominating the skyline, is more than 150 feet high. The Pope put Kazakhstan on the map of the Catholic world with a visit to Kazakhstan in 2001.

Lenin is Retired

New countries need new monuments, and Kazakhstan has erected its share of new symbols throughout the country. What always seemed incongruous was the looming presence of Lenin on Old Square in Almaty, in front of the old Parliament Building. (The parliament was exiled to Astana, providing Nazarbayev the opportunity to give the building to the new British-Kazakh Technical University, which trains students for the oil and gas industry.) The Square is now officially known as Astana Square. The statue of Lenin has been removed and replaced by a memorial, known as the Sniper Memorial.

The new statue remembers two daughters of Kazakhstan, Alia Moldagulova and Manshuk Mametova, who are known as war heroes for they lost their lives fighting for the Soviet Union in the "Great Patriotic War." Moldagulova was just 17 when she joined the Red Army and was trained as a sniper. She was credited with killing dozens of German soldiers. In January 1944, she was in a horrific battle near Pskov on the Western border of the Soviet Union. Despite being wounded, she continued to fight on until she was killed by the Germans. Manshuk Mametova was 19 when she volunteered for the Red Army. Not satisfied with being a nurse, she volunteered to become a machine gunner. She fell during the fighting for the city of Nevel. Both were posthumously awarded the title of Hero of the Soviet Union. The statue is in the tradition of war monuments of the Soviet era.

Sniper Statue replaced the Lenin Statue on Old Square.

One of the most dynamic tributes to the history of the Kazakh people is the new majestic Monument of Independence on New Square. New Square is now known as Republic Square, but the knockoff of the Lenin mausoleum is still there. In 1996, the Monument of Independence was dedicated on the Square. It is a magnificent work, although somewhat inaccessible, as the statue sits on a granite stele rising over the Square by some 90 feet. Nazarbayev was inspired by a visit to Luxor, Egypt and wanted the Monument of Independence to capture the beauty of ancient Egyptian art. And, in Egyptian tradition, on each side of the stele, there are ten reliefs reflecting various epochs in the history of the Kazakh people. A young warrior on a winged snow leopard crowns the monument. The warrior is a replica of "Gold Man," a young Saka prince from the fifth century BCE, discovered in an archaeological dig near Almaty in 1973. He gazes towards the Tien Shan Mountains, protecting the motherland from unseen enemies.

The winged snow leopard symbolizes beauty and power. At eye level are aphorisms in Kazakh, English, Russian, and ancient Turkish.

Independence Monument
on Republic Square.

Close-up of the Warrior on
the Snow Leopard.

One of the periods depicted on the stele is that of the 1986 disturbances, which took place on the Square. Off to the side of the monument, there is a new plaque which commemorates the disturbances:

"On this square on 17 December 1986, there occurred a democratic expression against the imposition of the command-administrative system. Let the memory of this event call peoples to rally for unity."

Republic Square is also home to the president's "Southern Residence" and one of two five-star hotels in Almaty, the Regent Ankara.

As the Russians Leave, the Foreign Investors Come: Milk and Cigarettes

The taxicab system has not significantly changed in the past ten years. During one of my return visits to Kazakhstan, I hailed a private cab one evening. I engaged the driver in a discussion, just as we were pulled over by a cop. The traffic cops are a strange breed in this part of the world. They simply stand at the side of the road and willy-nilly (read capriciously) motion with their white batons for cars to pull over. The driver told me to say that I was on an official visit to the tobacco factory. This explanation seemed strange at first...but then, after we were let off without even a fine, I listened more intently. The driver explained that he works for the recently privatized tobacco factory, the majority owner of which is Phillip Morris. Most people in this part of the world like talking about their salaries. I was curious, even though in the U.S. I know it is rude to inquire about someone's salary. I was justly rewarded for my curiosity with a rebuff. "It is a commercial secret," the driver responded. So I took a different tact. "What are the benefits?" I asked. "We get good discounts on milk and cigarettes in the factory's canteen." An interesting combination of products on which to offer discounts. Milk and cigarettes, indeed.

Kazakhstan had severe economic problems in the 1990s. Privatization faltered badly. Inflation went unchecked. The celebrated Chevron Tenghiz project stalled. The country was rife with corruption. Even now, in 2004, James Giffen, the CEO of merchant bank known as Mercator Corporation, is waiting trial in federal district court in New York, charged with paying $78 million in bribes to Nazarbayev and the former Prime Minister, Nurlan Balgimbayev, between 1995 and 2000.

But, despite some false starts and setbacks, the economy in Kazakhstan is on the move. The $2.6 billion pipeline from Tenghiz to the Russian Black Sea port of Novorossiysk commenced operations in December 2001. Foreign investment has crept up, mostly on the strength of Kazakhstan's wealth in natural resources. Kazakhstan attracted more than $2.5 billion of foreign direct investment in 2002, up from $1.2 billion in 1998. The gross domestic product (GDP) jumped at a sizzling rate of more than 13.5 percent in 2001 and 9.8 percent in 2002. And the economic prospects for Kazakhstan continue to be bright, particularly after the announcement in 2000 of a massive oil field on the Kazakhstan Caspian shelf. This field, known as the Kashagan field, may have as much as 13 billion barrels of recoverable oil, catapulting Kazakhstan into one of the world's leading oil exporters by 2010.

In a recently released report published by the United Nations Development Programme, Kazakhstan boasted the highest rating on a "human development index" of any Central Asian republic. The index combines scores on life expectancy, education, and per capita GDP. And with a per capita GDP of $5,870, Kazakhstan is three times as high as Uzbekistan and Kyrgyzstan but still below Russia. And this new wealth shows in Almaty and Astana.

Foreigners can now stay at one of two five-star hotels, the Regent Ankara Hotel and the Hyatt Regency/Rahat Palace. In what would have been anathema in the Soviet-era, the Regent Ankara Hotel on Republic Square is higher than the Presidential Palace. Up from Republic Square, towards the mountains, a building boom has produced new swank apartment complexes, and there is even a new Western-style mall, complete with escalators and an indoor skating rink. Astana opened a giant oceanarium in Astana—at a cost of $60 million, 83 percent of which was financed by the mayor's office. Astana also has built elite residential buildings.

But the booming economy has left large segments of the population behind. According to a World Bank report, as many as 38 percent of the population lives below the poverty line. Some predict a labor shortage if the economy continues to expand at a rapid rate. Hundreds of thousands emigrated from Kazakhstan, many Russian and ethnic Germans. The population fell to under 15 million (it had been almost 17 million) and is only recently on the rise again. Kazakhs are once again in the absolute majority, as 53 percent of the population is Kazakh, and only 30 percent Russian.

Disbanding of Parliament, Take 2, or Billiards and Parliamentarians, Strike That, Former Parliamentarians

Some of my friends in Kazakhstan think that life in Kazakhstan is dull until I come to town because somehow my visits have coincided with historic events. During one of my visits to Kazakhstan in March 1995, I learned that the Constitutional Court had just upheld the appeal of one parliamentarian who challenged the election results in her district. The Court ruled that the election was unconstitutional in this one district because the election violated the "one person one vote" principle of the Constitution.

This district was not the same size in terms of the numbers of voters as other districts. To have a valid election, 50 percent of the registered voters need to vote. But the ballots are of the old Soviet ilk: the voters have to cross out *those whom they do not want to vote for.* In the Soviet era, this made it easy to get 99.9 percent of the vote out, because there was only one candidate. Voters could simply pick up their ballot and throw it in the ballot box. If a voter were eyed marking the ballot, that meant, of course, he or she was an enemy of the people. It took great pains and courage to mark on the ballot. This system worked fine as it went in the Soviet era, but, when there are multiple candidates, the voters have to cross off all those whom they do not want to vote for.

What happens when a voter does not cross off any of the names or all but two of the candidates when the voter is supposed to vote for only one? The Election Commission gave all candidates one vote, thereby artificially increasing the number of voters and allowing the elections to be constituted. The Constitutional Court ruled that this practice was unconstitutional.

Nazarbayev challenged the decision and urged the Court to reconsider. In retrospect, it is not clear how sincere Nazarbayev was, because he reversed his decision within a day. He requested clarification whether this decision applied to just one district or the entire election. The Court responded that it applied to the entire election—even though the woman who had originally challenged the election only sought to challenge the election in one district, not in all 135 districts. And then there was the question of how this could apply to all 177 deputies when 42 had been elected—not on the basis of special election districts, but on the basis of administrative units within the country.

I visited a friend who lived in special housing reserved for high-level government officials. As is the custom, we had a generous dinner with his family. Between dishes, we retired to play some billiards in the recreation room, somewhat dissimilar to a recreation room in a condominium complex in the U.S. Billiards is a funny game in the former Soviet Union—and very different from the game of pool played at the fancy clubs in Manhattan.

In the former Soviet Union, the billiards table is larger than a standard pool table in the U.S. And the pockets are narrower. The billiard balls are larger than pool balls, and all of them are white. The players use cue sticks like in the U.S., but they can hit any ball into any other ball. A billiards game can take much longer to play than pool in the U.S.

When we arrived in the recreation room, there was already a game underway. There were five parliamentarians playing billiards, as they discussed the events of the week and the effect the decision would have on their tenure as members of parliament. At about the same time as their billiards game, President Nazarbayev was giving a news conference. One of the deputies hit one of the balls into another ball, and, after the balls stopped careening back and forth over the table, three white balls fell into various pockets. No one in the room had ever seen three balls fall in the pockets on one turn. It was a record. On the news later that night, we learned that Nazarbayev had declared that, "Parliament no longer exists." Another record, within 18 months two parliaments in Kazakhstan had been dissolved.

Preemptive Democracy Spreads in Central Asia

The brief flirtation with democracy in neighboring Turkmenistan and Uzbekistan ended in the mid-1990s, before it even got started. In what can only be described as a perversion of democratic principles, the presidents in those countries held referenda on extending the term of the president for four years without elections. Karimov in Uzbekistan received a Soviet-style 99.6 percent of the vote. He was quoted as saying that he was surprised at how much support he had in the population. Yeah, right. And which was the next country to follow this trend of democracy without elections? Kazakhstan. Nazarbayev, not wanting to feel left out of this authoritarian trend, adopted this preemptive democracy model. What is surprising is that Nazarbayev would likely have won election if he ran a democratic election. The referendum on April 29, 1995 gave Nazarbayev another four-year term without any opponent. Final returns reflected that 91 percent of the eligible voters participated in the election, and 95.5 percent voted in favor of extending the president's term. (After talking with friends and acquaintances, I could not find anyone who actually showed up to the polls.)

Constitutional Court—Strike That: Is That Anyway to Express Your Gratitude?

The young country with a dominating president turned to constitutional processes to attach a sense of legality to his desire to stay in the job for life. After the referendum assuring the president of a job to the year 2000, the president agitated scrapping the old Constitution, which was not even three years old. Nazarbayev invited "discussion" of this draft Constitution. On July 10, 1995, a majority of the members of the Constitutional Court wrote to Nazarbayev. The Court stated that "the draft shows a substantial strengthening of the bodies of the executive branch, and at the same a sharp weakening of the other two." The Court concluded, "The draft needs substantial reworking." (A minority of the Court weighed in with a letter of their own, excoriating the majority's selfish personal interests.)

A decision of the Constitutional Court had precipitated the dissolution of parliament. What was its just reward for providing the vehicle for Nazarbayev's decision? After the discussion, the final draft of the new Constitution eliminated the institution of the Constitutional Court. Instead, the Constitution created a weak Constitutional Council with little power or authority. Was that any way to express the president's gratitude?

No one waited with bated breath about the results of the referendum on the Constitution. The results showed that 90 percent of the eligible voters went to the polls, and 90 percent voted to "adopt" the new Constitution. And if you believe that the results comported with reality, then I have an air conditioner to sell for those warm December nights in Astana.

No Surprises Here: New Constitution Consolidates Presidential Powers

Did the new Constitution of 1995 read like the U.S. Constitution? The authors could not be charged with plagiarism. The Constitution was supposed to be modeled after the French Constitution; although there may be some French who would disagree. The Constitution contains some excellent provisions that would squarely fall within the principles of a Western democracy: presumption of innocence, no double jeopardy, an accused's right to legal assistance. Under the Constitution, freedom of speech is guaranteed and censorship is forbidden. Then there are the socialist-style guarantees, such as the right to rest and the right to health care.

The form of government is decidedly "presidential." The Constitution refers to checks and balances, but the president does most of the checking and balancing. He selects the premier; that's seems to be alright. He is the commander in chief; that sounds familiar. He selects seven members of the Senate (in which there are currently 39 members). The lower chamber of parliament, the Majilis, has 77 members. The Constitution allows the Senate and the Majilis to "delegate" to the president all legislative authority for one year. (That is a generous concession.) And members of parliament only get three excused absences. Otherwise, they are penalized, although the Constitution is silent about the measures that will be taken against absentees: walking backwards with one hand on your head and the other on your stomach. It doesn't say.

The 1995 Constitution raised the status of Russian, but just barely. Under the now defunct Constitution, Kazakh was the state language; and Russian was the language of discourse between nationalities. No one could figure out what that meant, but it was a boom for Russian-Kazakh translators. The Constitution of 1995 also finesses the issue. I have read many characterizations in newspapers in Kazakhstan, but I have not been able to find any report that captures what the text means. I do not think anyone knows. Here is my literal translation of the Russian version of the Constitution: "In state bodies and bodies of local authority, the Russian language shall be used officially on an equal footing with Kazakh."

The 1995 Constitution also allows amendments by the president, who can bypass the mechanism of a national referendum if he decides to submit them for review by parliament. In October 1998, he used this amendment authority to increase the president's term of office from five to seven years. The president orchestrated an election under these amendments on short notice, before any serious opposition could form. Nazarbayev received almost 82 percent of the vote in January 1999, a year before his term was up, but the Organization for Security and Cooperation in Europe (OSCE), which monitored the elections, declared that the elections fell "far short" of being democratic. (The Conference on Security and Cooperation in Europe was renamed in 1995.)

Presidential election, 1999:
Democracy?

In March 1997, I was in France with several members of the Constitutional Council of Kazakhstan, at the invitation of the Conseil Constitutionnel, the Constitutional Council of France. Our host at the Council was the President of the Council, Roland Dumas, former foreign minister of France. (After our visit, but not as a result of the visit, Dumas resigned from the Constitutional Council in a corruption probe. He was later convicted, but this conviction was overturned on appeal.) Dumas was supposed to be one of the advisers on the new Constitution in Kazakhstan. Dumas politely asked members of the Kazakhstani delegation about the Constitution in Kazakhstan. I interjected that he was supposed to be one of the leading advisers on that Constitution. He looked puzzled and exclaimed that that was news to him. One member of the Constitutional Council in Kazakhstan asked what other countries followed the French model of a Constitutional Council—there was a drawn silence as Dumas spoke in French to one of his colleagues and finally said, "I think Algeria is the only other country." And under his breath and not for translation, another member of the Constitutional Council of Kazakhstan said in Russian, "Looks like we are going to Algeria next year."

An Opposition Leader Drinks Italian Wine as Kazakhstan's Ambassador to Italy

Nazarbayev has tried to weaken and demoralize any opposition to his policies and, more importantly, his hold on power. One of the leading forces of democratic reform in the early 1990s was the poet, Olzhas Suleimenov. Many people looked at Suleimenov as the Václav Havel of Kazakhstan. Suleimenov founded the Nevada-Semipalatinsk movement and headed the People's Congress of Kazakhstan, which originally opposed the president. In 1995, Nazarbayev appointed Suleimenov as the Kazakhstan ambassador to Italy. Suleimenov accepted. Then in 2001, Suleimenov became Kazakhstan's permanent representative to UNESCO. The People's Congress since 1995 began to work with the government in constructive collaboration. The Party barely functions today.

In late 1998, I attended the trial of Petr Svoik, another opposition leader. Svoik was one of the leaders of the Azamat Party, which initially was uncompromising in its opposition to Nazarbayev. The authorities had refused to grant a permit for the group to hold a rally, but the gathering was held anyway, although no one spoke at the gathering. Svoik was charged with an administrative violation of participating in an unsanctioned demonstration. Svoik eloquently defended himself, citing the Constitution's right to gather, hold meetings, and demonstrations. The courtroom was packed; there was standing room only. There were a couple of television cameras, and the cameramen freely walked around the courtroom, sometimes approaching within inches of witnesses or even the judge. The judge nervously listened to the testimony and then retired so that she could make a decision. One member of the audience shouted at the judge as the judge retired to her office to consider a decision, "Why leave? It [the decision] is already ready." Not surprisingly, Svoik and his codefendants were found in violation of the law. Predictably, since 1998, Azamat has plotted a moderate position.

An even more serious challenge to Nazarbayev came from Akezhan Kazhegeldin, Nazarbayev's former prime minister, who had been a leader of the Republican People's Party of Kazakhstan. After Kazhegeldin announced his intention to run against Nazarbayev in the 1999 presidential election, Kazhegeldin was quickly tried and sentenced for a minor violation for participation in an unsanctioned demonstration. Because of this minor infraction, the Central Election Commission conveniently refused to confirm Kazhegeldin's eligibility to run. Kazhegeldin left the country.

And this soft authoritarianism has recently given way to harder authoritarianism. In September 2001, Kazhegeldin was tried *in absentia* for abuse of power, tax evasion, and weapons possession. He was sentenced to ten years of prison. Not surprisingly, Kazhegeldin has not returned to Kazakhstan. Other leaders opposed to Nazarbayev received similar harsh treatment. Several high-level government officials formed the Democratic Choice of Kazakhstan (DCK) at the end of 2001 and were subsequently removed from their positions. Two of DCK's founders, Galymzhan Zhakiyanov and Mukhtar Ablyazov, were arrested and convicted of abuse of power during their tenure as government officials. Freedom House, an international human rights group, ranks Kazakhstan as "not free," and Kazakhstan receives a "downward trend arrow due to increasing repression of the political opposition and media outlets."

A View to the Future—2030

In October 1997, Nazarbayev released a bold strategy for the future of Kazakhstan. The strategic plan, entitled "Kazakhstan—2030," outlines priorities for the country in seven major areas, including, for example, national security, economic growth, health, education, and welfare, among others. The plan attaches importance to the goal of domestic political stability—but not democracy. This omission is a clear choice of purpose as Nazarbayev trumpets stability as possibly the major driver to the development of Kazakhstan. Even economic growth will be achieved by "strengthening internal political stability and unity of society." The vision of Kazakhstan—2030 is to establish a long-term policy under which Kazakhstan and its people will live in prosperity, security, and improving well-being.

Nazarbayev predicts that Kazakhstan will emulate the experience of the "Asian Tigers" of Hong Kong, South Korea, Singapore, and Taiwan, which exhibited prodigious economic growth and rapid industrialization between 1965 and 1990. According to Nazarbayev's vision, Kazakhstan will become a Central Asian snow leopard, for which prosperity, security, and high living standards are integral parts of the landscape of the country. In his words,

"By 2030, I am certain that Kazakhstan will become a Central Asian snow leopard and will serve as an example for other developing countries. Tigers are not found here, and the snow leopard that inhabits our mountains is not familiar with the world community. Although a relative of the tiger in the animal world, the snow leopard nonetheless has differences. This will be a Kazakhstani snow leopard with its inherent elitism, independence, intellect, courage, nobility, bravery, and cunning. He will not attack first and will try to avoid direct confrontations. But if its freedom, habitat, or family is under threat, it will defend them at any cost. It must be lean and agile, not overweight or lazy: otherwise, it will not survive in the severe environment. It will be stubborn and persistent in conquering new heights, in purposefully searching for imperceptible but certain paths. The severe cold of threats should not frighten it, nor should it be made weak by the fever of opportunity. It will be wise in the upbringing of its family: defending them from uninvited visitors, giving them the tastiest morsels of food, caring for their health, education, and world view, and will prepare them for an early and independent life in the conditions of severe competition in any surroundings. It will strictly ensure that the water it drinks is not turbid, and the environment in which it lives and the water it breathes are improved. The Kazakhstani snow leopard will be possessed of Western elegance, multiplied by an advanced level of development, and Eastern wisdom and endurance."

Cynics only half jokingly suggested that Nazarbayev released the plan to show that the lofty goals could only be achieved under the skillful and watchful leadership of Nursultan Nazarbayev. The plan made a convincing case for a Nazarbayev presidency until 2030—unless, of course, he died first. Despite this criticism, Kazakhstan—2030 reflects leadership and purpose, which is part of the irony of Nazarbayev. If he were not such an authoritarian, he would be a good democrat.

The steppe has seen many leaders over the generations, and Nazarbayev's footsteps on the plains of Central Asia will not be the last etches into the landscape. Whether his vision will last against the penetrating wind of winter and the unforgiving sun of summer is a question for coming generations, for the steppe knows little of the limits of time or the bounds of space. Changes in Kazakhstan are over generations, not months or days. The time I was in Kazakhstan was the time that set the course for the new nation, a country hoping to emerge as a snow leopard.

Keith Rosten
St. Petersburg, Russia
August 2004

Index